COWAL &]

THE GUIDE]

(INCLUDING DUNOON, ARROCHAR & INVERARAY)

First published in 2013
by
Aird Trading (Publishing)
www.scotlandbooks.co.uk
www.scotlandguidebooks.co.uk

Authors: Lynne Woods & Doug Vickers

ISBN 978-0-9562126-6-5

Cover Picture: The Victorian Pier, Dunoon

INTRODUCTION

Welcome to "Cowal & Bute: The Guide Book" (including Dunoon, Arrochar & Inveraray), another in the series "See it....Do it....Don't Miss It....". The aim of each of these books is to help the visitor to do just that; to make the most of their stay in a given area. The fact that the area covered in this guide is perhaps not one of Scotland's most publicised and well known regions lends it a charm of its own. The joy of discovery is unspoilt by hoards of people round every corner and the main routes are seldom unpleasantly busy. Villages are linked by long stretches of peaceful, single track road meandering through wooded glens and past sparkling lochs to places which seem remote by road, having until recently depended on the sea as their main link with the outside world.

The purpose of this book, as with the others in the series, is to point out the major attractions but also to encourage you to explore "off the beaten track" and discover places you might otherwise not find. Because all our books are checked by local people before publication, we hope to provide an accurate picture of what is to be seen as well as the chance to discover some of Scotland's lesser-known delights.

The book is divided into sections, arranged in a logical order for touring either part or all of the area. Some sections are fairly short so that the whole book may be "dipped into" and used in the order which best suits your chosen route. The numbers on the map on page 4 correspond with the numbered sections of the book. Please note that our maps are not intended for precise navigation – their purpose is to indicate the general location of things mentioned in the text. Public toilets are not generally listed as many of these have been closed in recent years. In some places, village halls have made their facilities available. Elsewhere "comfort partnerships" have been agreed with hotels who make their toilets available to non-patrons – look out for signs. An index of place names for easy reference is included on page 71. On page 72 you will find a list of appropriate Ordnance Survey maps. Where used, six figure numbers prefixed by "GR" refer to grid references on such maps. Also on page 72 is a list of useful telephone numbers.

Whilst every effort has been made to ensure accuracy, things do change with the creation of new enterprises and the disappearance of others as people retire or move on, a fact for which the publishers cannot accept responsibility.

If this is the first time you have followed one of our guide books, we hope that it will enable you to make the most of your time around this peaceful corner of Scotland and that it creates a wish to return soon or to use one of our other books to explore a different area.

CONTENTS

(Red numbers refer to the area map on page 4.)

The Kyles of Bute, South of Colintraive

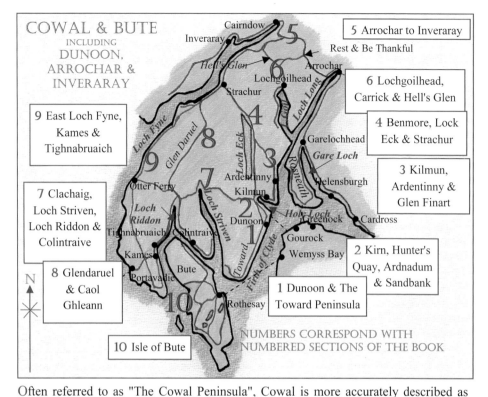

COWAL & BUTE
INCLUDING
DUNOON,
ARROCHAR &
INVERARAY

5 Arrochar to Inveraray

Rest & Be Thankful

6 Lochgoilhead, Carrick & Hell's Glen

9 East Loch Fyne, Kames & Tighnabruaich

4 Benmore, Lock Eck & Strachur

3 Kilmun, Ardentinny & Glen Finart

7 Clachaig, Loch Striven, Loch Riddon & Colintraive

8 Glendaruel & Caol Ghleann

2 Kirn, Hunter's Quay, Ardnadum & Sandbank

1 Dunoon & The Toward Peninsula

10 Isle of Bute

NUMBERS CORRESPOND WITH NUMBERED SECTIONS OF THE BOOK

Often referred to as "The Cowal Peninsula", Cowal is more accurately described as five separate peninsulas, bounded by Loch Fyne to the north and west, Loch Lomond and The Trossachs National Park to the east and the Firth of Clyde to the south east. Indented with spectacular sea lochs, it is an area of great contrasts: There are craggy peaks, extensive forests, sparkling lochs with remote and haunting shores and seaside resorts reminiscent of a more graceful age. At the foot of Cowal sits the island of Bute, close to the mainland but with its own distinctive identity. Whilst not strictly part of Cowal, Helensburgh and Rosneath are often visited as part of the same tour. A separate, smaller guide "Helensburgh & The Rosneath Peninsula: The Guide Book" (including Cardross, Garelochhead & Loch Long) covers that area.

Steeped in history, Cowal and Bute retain much evidence of early settlers and of more recent influence by the various clans. However, the area remains essentially unspoilt which is perhaps the reason why its varied habitats support such a wealth of wildlife, both in and out of the water.

The unique feel and character of the area can be largely attributed to two factors: Firstly, for many centuries its remoteness kept "outside" influences to a minimum and, secondly, when outside influence did arrive it was in a gentle manner. The single event which, above all other, opened up the area was the 19th century advent of the steam paddle ship. This new mode of transport provided a fast, safe and reliable link, not only with the city of Glasgow but also between remote settlements. The area became a popular Victorian destination – for day trips and summer holidays but also as a place from which wealthy businessmen could commute daily.

4

1. DUNOON & THE TOWARD PENINSULA

Dunoon

"**D**unoon is a cheerful little town" – said J.J. Bell in his 1932 guide "The Glory of Scotland". It remains a good description for one of Scotland's oldest parishes but which, until two hundred years ago, was little more than a fishing village. Victorian times brought the paddle steamer and Dunoon developed rapidly as a popular holiday resort. Activities centred around the Castle House Gardens and along the sea front, where several different boat hire companies operated. It also became home to wealthy Clyde businessmen who built elegant villas here, many of which are now hotels and guest houses. The town stretches around two bays with a gloriously long promenade. A quay was built in 1835 but replaced ten years later by a new pier. In 1868 Dunoon became a parliamentary

burgh. By the 1890s scores of paddle steamers called daily and the town also became one of the country's premier yachting venues. The pier was modified in 1954 when Dunoon had the first large car landing ramp.

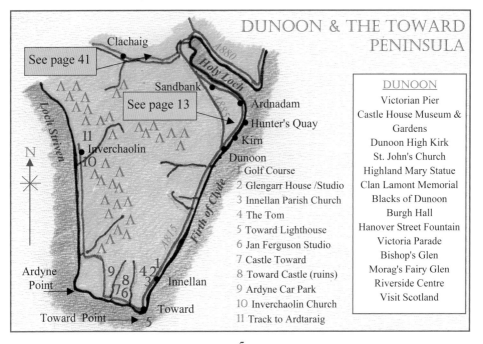

DUNOON & THE TOWARD PENINSULA

See page 41

See page 13

Clachaig
Sandbank
Ardnadam
Hunter's Quay
Kirn
Dunoon
1 Golf Course
2 Glengarr House /Studio
3 Innellan Parish Church
4 The Tom
5 Toward Lighthouse
6 Jan Ferguson Studio
7 Castle Toward
8 Toward Castle (ruins)
9 Ardyne Car Park
10 Inverchaolin Church
11 Track to Ardtaraig

Inverchaolin
Ardyne Point
Toward Point
Innellan
Toward

DUNOON
Victorian Pier
Castle House Museum &
Gardens
Dunoon High Kirk
St. John's Church
Highland Mary Statue
Clan Lamont Memorial
Blacks of Dunoon
Burgh Hall
Hanover Street Fountain
Victoria Parade
Bishop's Glen
Morag's Fairy Glen
Riverside Centre
Visit Scotland

The Pier Area

Victorian Pier: The original pier was extended in 1867. The year 1895 saw the official opening of the present Victorian pier with its pretty red roofed, wooden ticket office and waiting room. Today, a foot passenger service operates between Dunoon and Gourock. (For vehicle ferries – see Hunter's Quay page 14.)

Dunoon Pier

P.S. Waverley, the last sea-going paddle steamer, still calls at Dunoon in summer.

Queen's Hall is a large concert and events venue, opened in 1958 to replace an Edwardian building demolished a few years previously.

Castle Hill

Castle Hill dominates the sea front. An ancient 6th century stronghold, the site became a Lamont fortress during the 12th century before passing to the Campbells in the 14th century. Mary Queen of Scots stayed here in 1563. Very little remains of the castle as it was largely destroyed in 1685.

Castle House & Gardens

Castle House Museum: Gothic style Castle House was built in 1822 by David Hamilton for James Ewing, a Glasow provost. After having several other owners, the house and gardens were bought by the Burgh for public use. The house is now a museum, containing a wonderful and imaginatively presented collection of exhibits and tableaux detailing the history of Dunoon. These include a collection of models of Clyde steamers and sections on drovers, boat building, sail-making, toys of yesteryear and Cowal churches. There are also several unusual displays covering

Castle House Museum

Dunoon during WWII – including the sale of stirrup pumps during the War (£1) and surplus stock afterwards (7s 6d)! An audio visual display shows old postcards alongside present day versions of the same views. Several tableaux depict a Victorian Pier, the birthplace of Highland Mary and period furnished rooms.

Open Easter to Oct. Mon. – Sat. 10.30 – 16.00. Sun. 14.00 – 16.30.

Castle Gardens: Castle Hill viewpoint affords panoramic views over Dunoon's bays, the Victorian pier and beyond. In the gardens several interesting memorials include one to commemorate twenty-five years of co-operation with the US Naval base. Another memorial remembers John McLellan, "soldier, poet and composer of pipe music" who died in 1949.

Pitch and Put: A small pitch and put course is situated in the gardens.

The War Memorial is a beautiful sculpted Celtic cross remembering those who died in the two World Wars and, unusually, lists many of the campaigns.

Dunoon High Kirk is an early 19th century building in the "Decorated Gothic Revival" style. Gothic architecture dates from the mid 12th to mid 15th centuries. Gothic Revival was a Victorian move away from plainer, classical styles towards more ornate designs from the earlier era. Gillespie Graham's pointed gables and turrets, high ceilings and stained glass are typical of the style. Some of the gravestones are from the 13th century. Open Mon. – Sat. 10.30. -16.00. (seasonal)

The Braes Restaurant is a historic building, tastefully refurbished in a contemporary style with a choice of formal or informal dining. The carved oak bar is impressive and the balcony terrace enjoys spectacular views over the Clyde.

Highland Mary Statue: On Castle Hill is an imposing bronze statue of Robert Burns' fiancée who died before the marriage could take place - the betrothal having been sealed in the traditional way by exchanging bibles across a stream to signify that the love would endure as long as water ran and the Bible stayed true. Dunoon-born Mary caught a fever while nursing her sick brother and died in 1786 aged just 22. She was immortalised as Highland Mary (also Bonny Mary O'Argyll) in several of Burns' poems. The statue was erected in 1896, the 100th anniversary of his death.

Highland Mary

The Clan Lamont Memorial, at the head of Tom-a-Mhoid Road ("Hill of Justice"), remembers over two hundred Lamonts who were killed nearby by Clan Campbell in 1646.

Clan Lamont Memorial

Argyll Street

This is Dunoon's main shopping street, a lively bustling place lined with hanging baskets. There is a wide variety of places to eat and too many interesting, independent shops to mention each individually.

Argyll Gardens

Argyll Gardens is a pleasant sitting area at the seaward end of Argyll Street.

The Argyll Hotel: At the head of Argyll street, facing the sea, is the imposing Argyll Hotel, built to accommodate Victorian tourists and still offering a warm welcome to visitors. The Clyde Dining Room has a traditional Scottish menu. More informal dining is available in the bar or at Rio, the hotel's Italian restaurant.

Argyll Hotel

The Cinnamon Rooms serve Scottish and Asian food. (Black pudding pancakes and scallop chowder are particularly good!) Super choice of deserts. Reasonably priced early evening menu available.

The Tudor Tea Rooms & Curiosity Shoppes is a traditional tea room serving speciality teas and coffees all day. Below, a collection of shops sell various gifts and souvenirs including a "sweety" shop with old fashioned Scottish sweets.

Fishing Permits: Campbell's Paint & Hardware Shop sell fishing permits on behalf of The Dunoon & Disrict Angling Club for Lochs Tarsan & Loskin, Dunoon Resevoir and the rivers Masson, Finart, Ruel and Cur. Tel: 01369 704191

Blacks of Dunoon: The same family have been making all-butter Scottish shortbread since 1922, each successive generation serving their time as a baker. A small café serves traditional soups and, of course, shortbread.

Dunoon Mugs are found all over the UK but for the widest choice anywhere this has got to be THE place!

Bookpoint is a well-stocked bookshop with a wide range of books including many Scottish titles – a place to linger and browse!

The Flower Gallery sells a stunning array of plants and heathers. (Also mail order.)

The Burgh Hall dates from 1874. Like St. John's Church (see below), it was designed

The Burgh Hall

by Robert Bryden. The site was donated to the townsfolk by Mr. Macarthur Moir for municipal offices and a community hall. After The Queen's Hall took over this function in 1958 the Burgh Hall fell into disrepair. Happily, under the ownership of the John McAslan Family Trust, it has undergone extensive renovation and is now a community arts centre. At the front of the building is a Victorian drinking fountain with a carved hand of pink marble and the inscription "from a loving hand".

The Burgh Hall

St. John's Church, facing Argyll Street, is a large, Gothic building built in 1877 by Robert. Bryden. Its square tower, crowned with an octagonal spire, dominates the skyline. The interior is arranged in a semi circle with a central pulpit, choir gallery and unusual cast iron columns.

Hanover Street Fountain

Hanover Street Fountain: Just off Argyll Street, in a small garden, is a beautifully ornate drinking fountain embellished with black and gold lions and swans. Presented to the Burgh in 1899 by a former Provost, it is topped with a Provost's lamp. This is also a good place to admire the architecture of the back of the Burgh Hall.

Chatters Restaurant prides itself on being a "dining experience" rather than just another restaurant, serving the best of Scottish produce beautifully prepared and presented. Excellent wine list and a truly tempting pudding trolley. Garden dining, weather permitting.

West Bay

West Bay

Victoria Parade is a wide promenade, lined with hotels and guest houses and with spectacular views over the Clyde towards Inverkip and Wemyss Bay. Geese can often be seen on the shore.

The Gantocks: Off West Bay is a treacherous group of rocks marked by a 44' beacon, built in 1886 to warn shipping. Many ships have foundered here, including the paddle steamer Waverley in 1977 which was badly damaged when she grounded. Seals can often be seen basking on these rocks.

Crazy Golf: Adjacent to the ferry terminal is a crazy golf course.

The Yachtsman is a typical seaside café serving teas, coffees, snacks and home-baking. Hearty breakfasts (including vegetarian) available. Open all year.

The Esplanade Hotel is a large, welcoming, seafront hotel offering reasonably priced accommodation. Lunchtime soup and sandwiches available. Restaurant open evenings.

Play Area: At the southern end of Victoria Parade is a children's play area.

The Park Hotel is a comfortable, family run establishment Restaurant open 12.00 - 14.00 and 17.00 - 20.00. Open all year.

The Abbots Brae Hotel is a small luxurious hotel set in woodland gardens overlooking the Clyde. Rooms are named after local places, an individual history of each displayed in the rooms. Local produce, beautifully prepared and presented, is the keynote to dining here. Limited space for non resident dining. Booking essential. Tel: 01369 705021

Bishop's Glen was once the source of Dunoon's drinking water. In the 1870s the glen was dammed to create three reservoirs, one of which remains. Today the glen is a pleasant walk, accessed from the Kilbride Forest Car Park and linking with other Forestry Commission trails. By the bridge near the head of the reservoir are some interesting stone creatures – fashioned from piled rocks. A great place to let dogs

Morag's Fairy Glen

stretch their legs (but please remember to clean up after them!)

Morag's Fairy Glen is a wonderfully atmospheric hidden glen, accessed through a small arch in the wall across the road from the play area. Brown peaty water cascades down a series of waterfalls. A short way into the glen is a lovely sun-dappled glade with picnic tables. NB. The path can sometimes be slippery and care should be taken.

Morag's Fairy Glen

The Glenmorag Hotel was built in the early 19th century as a private mansion and still retains many original features. Its elevated position affords panoramic views over the Clyde. Restaurant open to non residents.

East Bay

East Bay

Visit Scotland: Dunoon's visitor information centre is manned by staff with a wealth of local information. There is also a gift shop selling books, maps and souvenirs. Free maps of Cowal available.

Seasons Coffee House is located in the Dunoon Baptist Church and is the place to find a seriously good snack. The home-made soups and cheese scones are excellent.

The Riverside Centre is a leisure complex with swimming pool, waterslides, sauna and café.

The Cowal Highland Gathering, held during the last week of August, is one of the largest of the annual Highland Games, the climax of which is the massed pipe bands of over three thousand pipers.

The Toward Peninsula

South of Dunoon the A815 hugs the western shore of The Firth of Clyde with fine views to Inverkip and Wemyss Bay. Several tracks lead into the forest and, for the energetic, to the summit of Corlarach Hill. (419m/1374') Beyond Toward Point the road meets the remote eastern shore of Loch Striven.

Innellan

South of Dunoon, Innellan House, built by the Campbells in 1650, once stood here. The village, like others along the Clyde, developed as a holiday resort from the mid 1840s. A pier built in 1851 was used until the 1970s but has now disappeared. The village also once had several shops, a bank, two hotels, four churches and its own gas and waterworks. Just offshore from Innellan is a small lighthouse perching on a dangerous outcrop of rock.

The Studio, Glengarr House: Brian Phillips paints delightfully quirky local scenes in vibrant colours with a hidden twist concealed somewhere in each piece. Visitors welcome but please telephone first: Tel: 01369 701590

The Tom: From Innellan forest tracks lead to The Tom, on which is a low mound believed to be a cairn dating from 2000BC. The Corlarach Loop Trail can also be accessed from here.

Innellan Golf Course is a nine hole course, created in 1891 on top of a hill. It is renowned for its dramatic sixth fairway which is divided by a gorge. Visitors welcome.

Innellan Post Office is also a general store, newsagents and off licence. Ferry tickets for sailings from Dunoon or Hunter's Quay can be purchased here.

Innellan Parish Church (Matheson Memorial Church), built in 1852, is a pretty building with a beautiful central stained glass window "The Light of The World" by Holman Hunt. The Rev. George Matheson who wrote "O Love That Wilt Not Let Me Go" was the minister here for eighteen years.

Jacob's Ladder is the name for the very steep path which joins Shore Road with North Campbell Road.

Toward

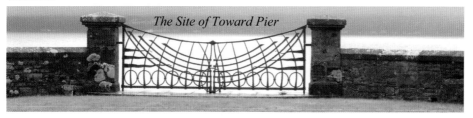

The Site of Toward Pier

Falkland Island Links: On the slopes above Port Stanley in the Falkland Islands 258 white heather plants from a farm at Toward were planted to commemorate the number of British men and women who died in the conflict.

Toward Lighthouse (now a private home) was built in 1812 by Robert Stevenson. It is 56' high and its light can be seen for 22 nautical miles. Nearby is a building which looks like a Victorian chapel but which, in fact, housed the machinery to power a foghorn which is still mounted on top.

Toward Lighthouse

Toward Point is a short walk along the shore beyond the lighthouse. The rocky nature of this stretch of coast is evident by the black and yellow cardinal buoy to warn ships of the dangers of coming too far inshore.

Toward Foghorn

Toward Pier was built in 1863 but only used until 1922. All that remains are two posts where it joined the land.

Picnic area: 1 km/0.6 miles west of Toward is a picnic area with superb views from the shingle shore.

Beyond Toward the A815 becomes a minor road which follows the shore round the headland and half way up the eastern shore of Loch Striven. On the southern edge of the peninsula is Toward Sailing Club. The building once housed the estate swimming pool. Toward Estate Office is a rather grand castellated building. Across the water is Rothesay on the Isle of Bute.

Jan Ferguson, Wildlife Portrait Artist, has her studio in the former estate smithy and post office. Self taught, she achieves such exquisite detail that her work really has to be seen to be believed. Exhibiting at various

Jan Ferguson

Oystercatchers

Jan Ferguson

venues during the season, her work is also internationally appreciated. To visit the studio please telephone first. Tel: 01369 870346

Castle Toward is a castellated mansion built in 1821 by architect David Hamilton for a former Lord Provost of Glasgow. During WWII it became a War Office Combined Operations Centre. It is now an outdoor training centre. In the grounds are two walled gardens.

Toward Castle: In the grounds of the outdoor centre are the ruins of an ancient castle built by the Lamonts in 1475. A path leads from the car park into the woods to the ruins.

Ardyne Point: Beyond the estate office is a magnificent oak tree at the start of a signposted path to the shore and Ardyne Point, from where there are views over Loch Striven to the Kyles of Bute.

Ardyne Car Park has information boards and is a popular starting point for a circular walk through the forest via Innellan.

Loch Striven: Its sheltered aspect makes this an ideal naval base. During WWII, prototypes of Barnes Wallis's famous bouncing bomb, used in The Dambusters raid, were tested here. It is now the site of an MOD refuelling depot, the public road passing between high fences topped with razor wire. Beyond the depot the road is lined with blackberries and meanders between shore and forest with spectacular views up Loch Striven.

Inverchaolain, meaning "mouth of the narrow stream", nestles below the conical shaped Black Craig to the east. It was once a thriving community but, as with many other glens in Scotland, the 18th century saw sheep become more profitable than people.

Black Craig

Inverchaolain Church

Inverchaolain Church is delightful. It was built in 1912 to replace one built a hundred years earlier which had burned down but two even older churches had existed here. Although no longer holding regular services, the church is open to visitors. The Lamonts have been dominant in this area since Norse times, many of them interred in the graveyard. Inside the church hand-held information tablets are available. Behind a grill near the altar can be seen pewter communion plates and goblets gifted in 1842 by Lady Lamont.

Pewter Communion Plates

The Old Manse, behind the church, was built in 1730 and is a listed building (now holiday accommodation).

Beyond the church, the public road continues a further 2 km/1.2 miles before ending at the lodge to the Glen Striven Estate. However, it is possible to continue on foot along the track which runs to Ardtaraig near the head of the loch.

2. KIRN, HUNTER'S QUAY, ARDNADAM & SANDBANK

The A815 north follows the coast from Dunoon, through Kirn to Hunter's Quay then round the headland at Sandbank to meet Holy Loch before joining the A885.

Kirn

Kirn, now an extension of Dunoon, was once a thriving village with a pier built in 1845 and featuring attractive red brick buildings. There are pleasant seafront gardens, a number of shops and cafés and a well stocked convenience store. The foreshore is a "pebble hunter's paradise" and a favourite haunt of oyster catchers and herons.

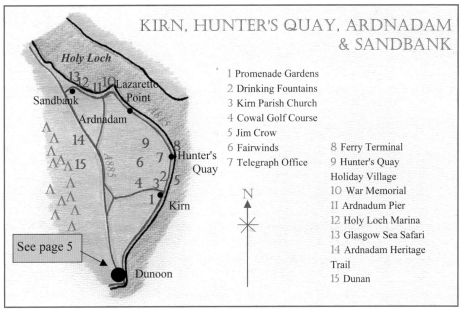

KIRN, HUNTER'S QUAY, ARDNADAM & SANDBANK

1 Promenade Gardens
2 Drinking Fountains
3 Kirn Parish Church
4 Cowal Golf Course
5 Jim Crow
6 Fairwinds
7 Telegraph Office
8 Ferry Terminal
9 Hunter's Quay Holiday Village
10 War Memorial
11 Ardnadum Pier
12 Holy Loch Marina
13 Glasgow Sea Safari
14 Ardnadam Heritage Trail
15 Dunan

See page 5

Promenade Gardens: These are delightful with picnic tables, floral displays in rowing boats and a wonderful collection of oversized games including snakes and ladders (a spinning tyre replaces a dice), a giant chess board and a vertical noughts and crosses.

Victorian Drinking Fountains: Along the promenade these curious, ornate wrought iron structures bear the inscription "Keep the pavement dry".

Kirn Parish Church is an imposing early 20th century, red sandstone building. It was designed in "Romanesque" style by architect P. MacGregor Chalmers (1859 – 1922) and combines curves and angles in a pleasing way.

Cowal Golf Course is an eighteen hole course designed by James Braid. Visitors welcome.

Jim Crow

Kirn Shore

Jim Crow: On the foreshore a massive boulder deposited here by a glacier has been painted to resemble a crow! The nearby rocks are attractively marked with wavy lines – the result of glacial scarring.

Hunter's Quay

Western Ferries Terminal

Palm trees and pampas grass give an almost tropical feel to Hunter's Quay which was named after James Hunter of Hafton House who built a stone pier here in 1828. Once the scene of many yachting regattas, there are numerous hotels and guest houses overlooking the Clyde. A frequent service operates between Hunter's Quay and McInroy's Point near Gourock. Booking not necessary.

Fairwinds (George Street) is a beautiful garden, created in the 1950s and for the past forty years lovingly tended and developed by the same owner. It is a blaze of colour throughout the year. Trees include maple, copper beech and a spectacular 20' high flame red acer in the middle of the lawn. Open all year.

The Royal Marine Hotel

Hunter's Quay Hotel is a former Victorian sea front villa amidst lawns and woodland and offering luxury accommodation and fine dining.

The Royal Marine Hotel, a magnificent building designed by architect Leonard Knox Watson, was once the venue of The Royal Clyde Yacht Club with HRH Albert Edward Prince of Wales as a member. A large stained glass window by J. W. Guthrie on the main staircase features a small panel donated by the Prince and depicting a crown. The present hotel is comfortable and welcoming with a lovely dining room overlooking the Clyde. Gillies Bar offers less formal, all day dining.

Telegraph Office: At the entrance to The Royal Marine Hotel a tiny, quaint black and white building was one of Scotland's first telegraph offices. It was built for use by The Prince of Wales when he stayed at the hotel. It now houses Coffee Ahoy which serves freshly ground coffee, excellent sandwiches and packed lunches. Open daily 07.00. – 17.00.

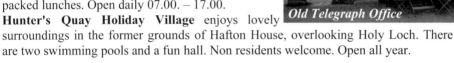
Old Telegraph Office

Hunter's Quay Holiday Village enjoys lovely surroundings in the former grounds of Hafton House, overlooking Holy Loch. There are two swimming pools and a fun hall. Non residents welcome. Open all year.

Ardnadam

Holy Loch possibly gained its name when a boat carrying sacred soil from Jerusalem to Glasgow Cathedral sank nearby and so "blessed" the loch. An alternative theory cites St. Mun or St. Columba who built chapels on the shore. Holy Loch was the scene of much wartime activity. (See page 16.)

Holy Loch

Lazaretto Point: "Lazaretto" means a maritime place of quarantine. In the early 19th century cargoes of cloth would be stored in vessels temporarily moored offshore to prevent disease being imported along with the cloth! Yellow flags indicated that no one should approach. Glen Cottage was originally the customs house. Until the 1960s a ferry ran from here to Kilmun and Strone. A tall circular tower commemorates the dead of two World Wars, including the crews of six submarines which left Holy Loch and did not return. The railings by the memorial are linked by anchor chain with anchors at either end.

War Memorial: The elegant circular memorial here was dedicated in 1922 to remember those men from Ardnadam and Sandbank who lost their lives in WWI. After WWII a further plaque was added for those killed then, along with the names of submarines which sailed from Holy Loch and were lost. In 2012, a further plaque was erected to remember the "Cockleshell Heroes" of Operation Frankton who paddled canoes to fix mines to German ships in Bordeaux Harbour.

Ardnadam Pier

Ardnadam Pier, built in 1858 to serve steamers bringing visitors from Glasgow, is

60m (200') long - the longest on the Clyde. During WWII this was a Royal Naval base where "liberty ships" were loaded - mass produced cargo ships used in the Allied merchant fleet.

Beyond Sandbank was a decoy shipyard intended to attract bombing and protect the real one. Between 1961 and 1992 American Navy Polaris submarines were based in Holy Loch. The pier is still in use, large vessels mooring here to load timber. On the car park are several information boards with pictures of days gone by. Note also the attractive planters featuring boats.

Sandbank

The village was once no more than a few fishermen's cottages. Drovers and other travellers passed through. Later, the village grew when a hotel was built. During the Napoleonic Wars there was a cooperage to provide barrels for the nearby gunpowder mill. At one time there was also a distillery. When this closed the site became a boatyard, building many famous yachts and several RNLI lifeboats.

Sandbank

Children's Playground: There is a nice play area just beyond the car park.

Holy Loch Marina was once a boatyard. For over a hundred years wooden vessels, including yachts, were built here. It is now a leisure marina offering full marine facilities and includes a coffee shop and snack bar.

Glasgow Sea Safari, at the marina, offers exhilarating wildlife-spotting trips on the Clyde in a rigid inflatable boat. To book Tel: 07557 905043 www.glasgowseasafari.com

Ardnadam Heritage Trail (signposted from the A885) is a fascinating walk through ancient woodland with beech, hazel, rowan and a single juniper tree. Many tree trunks are attractively adorned with ferns. Look out also for red squirrels. Layers of history unfold at every bend. An excellent leaflet (available from Visit Scotland) points out the site of an iron age roundhouse, historical enclosures and dykes, coppiced trees and much more. Information boards show how the settlements would have looked when they were inhabited. The path continues to the top of Dunan for panoramic views.

Coppiced Woodland

Picnic area: A small loch-side car park and picnic area (with public BBQ) is an excellent place for spotting mute swans, eider ducks, ringed plovers, oystercatchers, herons and many other wading birds. Information boards give details of local wildlife and an interesting history of the village.

The Holy Loch Inn has a real "village pub" feel to it. Dog friendly. Food served.

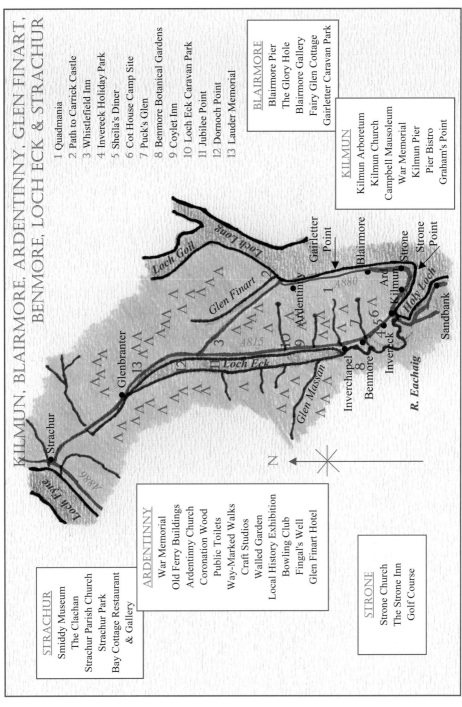

KILMUN, BLAIRMORE, ARDENTINNY, GLEN FINART, BENMORE, LOCH ECK & STRACHUR

1 Quadmania
2 Path to Carrick Castle
3 Whistlefield Inn
4 Invereck Holiday Park
5 Sheila's Diner
6 Cot House Camp Site
7 Puck's Glen
8 Benmore Botanical Gardens
9 Coylet Inn
10 Loch Eck Caravan Park
11 Jubilee Point
12 Dornoch Point
13 Lauder Memorial

BLAIRMORE
Blairmore Pier
The Glory Hole
Blairmore Gallery
Fairy Glen Cottage
Gairletter Caravan Park

KILMUN
Kilmun Arboretum
Kilmun Church
Campbell Mausoleum
War Memorial
Kilmun Pier
Pier Bistro
Graham's Point

STRACHUR
Smiddy Museum
The Clachan
Strachur Parish Church
Strachur Park
Bay Cottage Restaurant & Gallery

ARDENTINNY
War Memorial
Old Ferry Buildings
Ardentinny Church
Coronation Wood
Public Toilets
Way-Marked Walks
Craft Studios
Walled Garden
Local History Exhibition
Bowling Club
Fingal's Well
Glen Finart Hotel

STRONE
Strone Church
The Strone Inn
Golf Course

The A880 leaves the A815 north of Sandbank to follow the northern shore of Holy Loch, round the headland at Strone Point to Loch Long and on to remote Ardentinny. A minor road then winds up through Glen Finart, rejoining the main road north alongside Loch Eck.

Holy Loch - Northern Shore

Kilmun

Kilmun Arboretum is a beautiful forest with way-marked paths meandering between groves of trees from around the World. It was established by the Forestry Commission in the 1930s and 40s to investigate which species were best suited to Scotland's west coast climate. Over two hundred and fifty species thrive here, along with wildlife including red squirrels and Scottish crossbills.

Kilmun Church: Mundas, Abbot of Argyll, is thought to have established a church here, during the 9th century. However, recent excavations have revealed an 8th century grave with a Bishop's cross, thought to be that of Mun. Since the 14th century the church has been closely associated with the Campbells. The present tower dates from the 15th century although most of the current church was built in 1841 with later extensions. The organ is driven by a hydraulic pump, one of only two such in Scotland. The church vault contains the remains of The Marquis of Argyll who was beheaded in 1661 for treason. His head was carried around the kingdom as a warning to others and not laid with the rest of him until three years later! The graveyard is truly fascinating: Elizabeth Blackwell, the first female doctor, is interred in the grounds with a headstone detailing her life. Another grave is that of a shepherd, James Grieve, who lived to be one hundred and eleven! An unusual water tap takes the form of a lion with a pipe in its mouth.

Kilmun Church & Mausoleum

Elizabeth Blackwell's Grave

The Campbell Mausoleum dates from around 1790, replacing an earlier chapel. Prior to this Campbells were interred in the vault beneath the church floor. In 1890 the mausoleum was renovated and the cast iron dome added by The Marquis of Lorn (later the 9th Duke) who was married to Queen Victoria's daughter Louise. Within the mausoleum, a statue of her father-in-law, the 8th Duke, was made by Louise on his death in 1900. Excavations have revealed many artefacts including a carved ceremonial boar's head - the symbol of Clan Campbell. A museum and information point are being developed.

War Memorial: By the church entrance stands a war memorial for Kilmun, Strone, Blairmore and Ben More.

Kilmun Pier: Kilmun was the home of 19th century engineer David Napier, champion of steamboat travel. He built the pier in 1827 as part of a scheme to develop a steamboat service on Loch Eck. Passengers would alight at Kilmun to be transported along a newly built road to Lock Eck for the onward journey to Inveraray. The pier closed in 1971. A quaint post office at the end of the pier is now holiday accommodation.

The Pier Guest House & Bistro serves coffee and cakes, lunches and dinners in a light and airy dining room overlooking the pier. There is also a gallery and gift shop.

Graham's Point is a delightful place with a modern stone circle, sculptures, playground, picnic area, a public barbecue and information boards written in

The Pier Bistro, Kilmun

Poetic Tribute to David Napier

verse! One describes the loch and its wildlife while another, illustrated with charming pictures, tells the story of David Napier and his quest to get people to explore the Clyde. A granite obelisk, erected in 1906, commemorates the life and work of James Duncan who did much to improve the Benmore Estate.

Strone

Strone is a pretty village with a post office, pier and villa-type houses with decorative iron verandas and balconies.

Strone Inn

Strone Church was built by Peter MacGregor Chalmers who was responsible for many early 20th century churches. It replaced a 19th century church on the same site and contains some lovely stained glass windows

The Strone Inn is a welcoming, old fashioned lochside inn with a beer garden. The entrance is adorned with two quirky sailor figures and marine artefacts decorate the walls of the traditional bar.

Blairmore & Strone Golf Course (nine holes) was designed by Braid and opened in 1896. Visitors welcome – honesty box by the clubhouse.

Blairmore:

Beyond Strone Point the road meets Loch Long. Blairmore is a leisurely place to linger. As with other shore villages, it developed as a popular place to holiday when steamers opened up the remoter parts of the Clyde.

Blairmore Pier

Blairmore Pier, originally built in 1855, has been restored by The Friends of Blairmore Pier Trust and is available for berthing, as well as being popular with anglers. Swans can often be seen here.

The Old Ticket Office, also restored, offers unusual holiday accommodation.

The Glory Hole is a bric-a-brac shop, selling books, toys and other interesting bits and pieces.

Blairmore Gallery is a welcoming place combining a Fairtrade coffee shop with an art gallery showcasing the work of many Argyll artists.

Fairy Glen Cottage: Elizabeth Bruce creates unique, contemporary still-lifes and landscapes in a variety of media including acrylics, lino prints and etchings. Visitors welcome but please telephone first: Tel: 01369 840219

Gairletter Caravan Park enjoys a stunning shore location with static caravans and self catering cottage accommodation.

Quadmania!

Quadmania is a superb facility offering archery, clay pigeon shooting and quad trekking, the only five star quad amenity in Scotland. Helmets and wellies provided. Booking advisable. Tel: 01369 810246

Stronchullin Holiday Cottages offer excellent self catering accommodation in tranquil surroundings with fabulous views.

The stretch of road beyond Gairletter Point is particularly attractive, meandering beside Loch Long amongst mature oak trees, sycamore, birch, alder and rhododendrons.

Ardentinny

This is a pretty village with a pleasant sandy beach and a row of listed 18th century white cottages stretching along the shore, one of which has an intriguing figure sculpted on the end. The peaceful loch shore is a lovely place to sit.

Ardentinny

The Ardentinny Hotel is a listed 18th century building, originally a drovers' inn as well as accommodating travellers en route to Coulport by ferry. Many original features survive, including the stone stairway.

Ardentinny War Memorial stands to the left of the road in memory of local men who lost their lives.

Old Ferry Buildings & Slipway: A ferry once operated between here and Coulport, summoned from the other side by lighting a beacon. During the season this is a popular place with visiting boats.

Ardentinny Church, a listed building, was built by The Laird of Glen Finart in 1838 and is of a simple, elegant design with a small bellcote at the front.

Ardentinny Church

Public Toilets: In the car park are some extremely well cared-for public toilets.

Coronation Wood was planted by the children of the village in 1953 to commemorate the coronation of Queen Elizabeth II. It has recently been restored and is now an inviting place to walk or sit. The original entrance plaque remains.

Forestry Commission Walks: Several walks begin from the car park, including a circular riverside walk following the River Finart up the glen. Another walk leads to the Laird's Grave where the Laird, Archibald Douglas, is buried. From where the road leaves the shore, it is possible to continue along an upgraded footpath to Carrick Castle (see page 39).

Freda Waldapfel, a talented artist and landscape gardener, has a studio in one of the Swedish houses, built in the 1950s to house forestry workers.

Bill Williamson Ceramics: From a garden studio Bill Williamson creates whimsical ceramic sculpted figures and raku fired thrown pots. To visit Tel: 01369 810238

The Walled Garden, once part of the Glenfinart Estate, is now owned by Ardentinny Community Trust and houses a community orchard and vegetable gardens as well as quiet contemplative areas. The curved end wall, a listed structure, is one of only two such in the country. Built into the walls are propagation ovens.

The Village Hall was built in 1906 in memory of Henry Pige Leschalles, one time owner of Glenfinart. In the hall is a local history exhibition. If not open, Tel: 01369 810385

Ardentinny Bowling Club welcomes non members.Tel: 01369 810307

Glen Finart Caravan Park (static caravans only) is in the grounds of what used to be Glenfinart House, a stone tower being all that remains of the original building. A lovely waterfall plunges beneath the road by the entrance.

Roadside Waterfall

Fingal's Well. This was created by Laird Archibald Douglas to water his horse, Fingal. Fingal was with the laird in the Crimean War. It is said that when the horse died he was buried on the hill near his master.

Glen Finart:

Via Ardentinny, this is a picturesque alternative to the main road between Dunoon and Strachur. The road follows the bottom of the glen, a glorious carpet of bluebells in the spring, before climbing steeply between majestic, heather-clad ridges. Many tracks lead into the forest.

The Glen Finart Hotel: The Stalkers' Restaurant serves "homely" food with an emphasis on personal service. Specialities include venison, kangaroo, bison and ostrich. Open daily from 12.00.

Loch Eck: As the road descends, there are superb views down to Loch Eck, known to be the only loch other than Loch Lomond where the rare powan fish lives naturally. Loch Eck is 10 km/ 6.25 miles long but never more than 600m/ 666 yards wide. (See page 23.)

The Whistlefield Inn: Initially dating from 1455, much of the present building originated as a mid 17th century drovers' inn, with Victorian and Edwardian additions to accommodate the new "tourist trade". The inn continues to be a welcoming place with accommodation, a varied menu and real ales.

4. BENMORE, LOCH ECK & STRACHUR
(SEE MAP ON PAGE 17)

Heading north from Dunoon, the A885 joins the A815 to follow the eastern shore of Loch Eck.

Invereck

Invereck Countryside Holiday Park enjoys an idyllic location at the foot of Loch Eck on the banks of the River Eachaig.

Sheila's Diner is open for most of the year for eat-in or take-away meals, hot rolls, drinks etc. and a weekly Sunday roast.

Cot House Camp Site is clean, well kept, reasonably priced and welcomes tents and touring caravans.

Cot House Services: In addition to fuel, there is a well stocked shop selling groceries, fresh fruit & vegetables, wines & spirits, newspapers etc. as well as ferry tickets for Gourock.

Puck's Glen is signposted to the right, north of the A815/A880 junction. It is a short but atmospheric walk through a gorge with many waterfalls, steps and bridges. The path, originally built by the Youngers brewing family, links up with other, longer routes.

Benmore Botanical Garden

Benmore Botanic Garden is an outpost of The Royal Botanic Gardens, Edinburgh. Here the climate ideally suits rhododendrons, of which over two hundred and fifty species can be seen. Some of Britain's tallest trees grow here along with plants and shrubs from all over the World. There are 9.5 km/6 miles of paths, many of them wheelchair and buggy friendly. The visitor centre has a café and shop.

(Photograph courtesy of Benmore Botanical Garden.)

Lock Eck

Loch Eck ("loch of the horse") is a long, ribbon-shaped loch, 10.3 km/6.25 miles long, no more than 0.6 km/660 yards wide but one of Scotland's deepest lochs – 140m/460' in places. It nestles between steep ridges and peaks dominated by Ben Mhor (741m/2430') to the west. Its shores are fringed with trees including majestic Scots pines.

Inverchapel stands just south of where the River Eachaig flows out of Loch Eck. The Forestry Commission car park here is a popular starting point for various walks, including The Loch Eck Loop.

The Coylet Inn, originally a 17th century coaching inn called The Loch Eck Hotel, enjoys a spectacular location on the loch shore ("Coylet" means a wooded inlet) with boats available for hire to take full advantage of the setting. Food available daily from midday.

Loch Eck Caravan Park is a holiday park in a beautiful location on the banks of the River Eachaig at the southern end of Loch Eck. (No tourers or tents.)

Jubilee Point, on a small promontory signposted from the road, is a secluded picnic site with lovely views up the loch. The pine trees by the car park are over 170 years old. Red squirrels can often be seen here.

Jubilee Point

Just north of Jubilee Point, a minor road leads into Glen Finart (see page 22) which links Lochs Eck and Long. A short distance from the junction is The Whistlefield Inn. (See page 22.)

Mileposts: Look out for large, attractive cast iron mileposts along this stretch of the A815.

Dornach Point is a Forestry Commission picnic site. Just offshore is a tiny island where, according to legend, Robert the Bruce was once entertained. It is thought to be a "crannog", an artificial island upon which a dwelling would have been built.

The Lauder Monument (signposted from the road) was erected in 1921 by famous Scottish entertainer Sir Harry Lauder in memory of his son who was killed in WWI. The song "Keep Right On To The End Of The Road" was written later by Sir Harry. The Invernoaden car park is just beyond the sign for the monument.

Glenbranter Forest was leased from Sir Harry Lauder to the Forestry Commission in 1921, Glenbranter village developing in the 1950s to house foresters. There are various walking and cycling trails, an information room and toilets. In addition to recreation, the forest is managed for timber, as is evident by wood stacks, new plantings and the timber lorries to be seen on the road. (A large wooden model of one can be seen outside a cottage just north of here!)

Strachur

The village was originally called "Kilmaglas" - "Maglas" being a version of St. Molaise. Principal landowners in this part of Argyll were Campbells and MacLachlans.

The Smiddy Museum, with its large forge, was the village smithy from the 18th century until the 1950s. The interior remains almost unchanged from that time so provides a genuine glimpse into the past. At the rear is a gallery and craft shop selling locally made items including wooden toys. Open daily 13.00 – 16.00. Easter – Sep.

The Smiddy

The Clachan was built in 1804 but only became a public house in 1979. Prior to that it was a bakery, the large ovens having occupied what is now the pool room.

Ancient Grave Slabs

Strachur Parish Church was built in 1789 and renovated in the early 20th century. Quite remarkable are eleven ancient grave slabs, one dated 1698 but the others thought to be from the 14th and 15th centuries, found in an older burial ground. They have been incorporated into the outside wall of the present church. The interior is of a simple design with a wooden gallery. A circular stained glass window features an unusual geometric design.

Strachur House was largely built in the late 18th century for General John Campbell whose descendents still own the house. Chopin visited in 1848.

Graveyard, Strachur

Strachur Park was laid out in 1782 by General Campbell and is a planned woodland landscape with walks, ornamental bridges and a lochan, renowned for its reflections in autumn. Walkers are welcome to explore the grounds. A leaflet is available from the smiddy. The flower gardens are open on selected dates only.

Bay Cottage is a welcoming licensed tea room, general store, newsagents and post office situated on the A866 at Strachur Bay. Home cooking & baking served daily. Bob Brown paintings on display (see page 49.) Open till 19.00 during the summer months. (Booking recommended. Tel: 01369 860221)

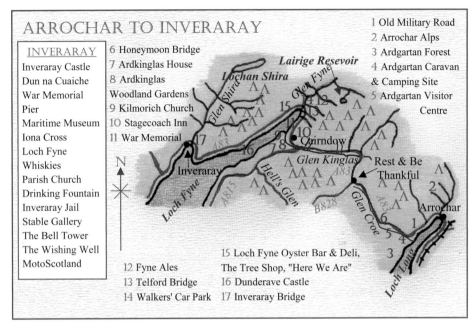

ARROCHAR TO INVERARAY

INVERARAY	
Inveraray Castle	6 Honeymoon Bridge
Dun na Cuaiche	7 Ardkinglas House
War Memorial	8 Ardkinglas
Pier	Woodland Gardens
Maritime Museum	9 Kilmorich Church
Iona Cross	10 Stagecoach Inn
Loch Fyne	11 War Memorial
Whiskies	
Parish Church	
Drinking Fountain	
Inveraray Jail	
Stable Gallery	
The Bell Tower	
The Wishing Well	
MotoScotland	

1 Old Military Road
2 Arrochar Alps
3 Ardgartan Forest
4 Ardgartan Caravan & Camping Site
5 Ardgartan Visitor Centre

12 Fyne Ales
13 Telford Bridge
14 Walkers' Car Park
15 Loch Fyne Oyster Bar & Deli, The Tree Shop, "Here We Are"
16 Dunderave Castle
17 Inveraray Bridge

Arrochar & Tighness

Originally part of the Parish of Luss, this became an independent parish in 1659. Samuel Lewis, writing in 1846, described Arrochar as a place ...." *much resorted to by tourists on account of the peculiar and numerous attractions which it presents, as well as from the excellence of the inns, the good order of the roads, and other advantages."* There are several theories behind the name: "Arachor" was an area of land which could be ploughed by eight oxen in a year and "Arroquhar" was Celtic for "hilly country". Situated at the head of Loch Long, Arrochar and Teighness were no more than a few scattered houses until the mid 18th century. A military road was built between Dumbarton and Inveraray in 1746 and then, in the 1800s, steamers arrived. Arrochar became part of the classic "Three Lochs Tour" (Lochs Lomond, Goil and Long) and in 1849 Queen Victoria visited in the royal yacht. Tourists arrived and departed by water, coal and lime were brought here by ship and wool was exported. The Cowal Way runs through Arrochar.

The Head of Loch Long

The Arrochar Alps shield the heads of Lochs Long and Goil and contain five Munros (mountains over 3000') including Beinn Ime at 1011m/3316'. The most well known mountain, although not a Munro, is Ben Arthur (The Cobbler) which, at 884m/2890' is a "Corbet."

The Village Inn (1872), once the manse, is a popular loch-side inn with accommodation, real ale and a good restaurant. In the bar are a set of huge bellows from an old workshop and an interesting model of the inn. At low tide sea birds forage on the nearby shore for mussels and other delicacies.

The Village Inn

Mansefield Studio exhibit hand-made ceramics and other Scottish crafts. Tom Butcher is renowned for his ceramic sculptural pieces and domestic stoneware. Open all year Mon. – Sat. 10.30 – 17.30.

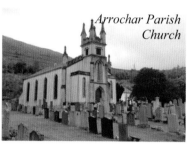

Arrochar Parish Church

Tighness Stores sells newspapers, wines & spirits, groceries, fresh fruit & vegetables, soft drinks and fresh coffee.

The Parish Church was built in 1847 overlooking the loch near the site of an earlier 1733 kirk, the ruins of which may still be seen. Before 1847 the church bell hung in a tree. By the end of the 20th century the church was much in need of repair and was extensively refurbished.

Three Villages Community Hall is a vibrant place with visitor information, welcoming Saturday coffee mornings, Wi Fi, a badminton court, table tennis tables and a fascinating display of local history. Reception usually manned 10.00 – 16.00.

Three Villages Café serves a varied menu with fresh coffee and home baking. Fish suppers and Scotch Pie suppers are especially popular.

3 Villages Café

The Pit Stop Take-away is attached to the café. Take-away food and Scottish ice cream.

The Arrochar Hotel dates from the 19th century and is a comfortable hotel with a lounge enjoying stunning views over the loch. Well behaved dogs are welcome.

The Claymore Hotel, catering mainly for coach parties, was originally the seat of Clan McFarlane.

The War Memorial, on the Tarbet road, takes the form of a simple Celtic Cross.

Braeside Stores & Post Office is one of those wonderful places which seem to sell a bit of everything – newspapers, fishing tackle, souvenirs, confectionary and hot coffee.

The Ben Arthur Bothy has a bar, lounge, pool table, Wi Fi and lochside patio. Reasonably priced accommodation also available.

Mini2You has an unusual combination of goods; dolls' houses, fresh fruit and vegetables and Airfix models.

The Jubilee Well, opposite the shops, was built to celebrate Queen Victoria's Jubilee and renovated in 1977 for Queen Elizabeth II's Silver Jubilee.

The Jubilee Well

Arrochar Chippy is more than its name suggests, serving teas, coffees and a wide range of fast foods, including spicy beanburgers.

The Village Shop is another "Aladdin's Cave" with hot take-aways, sandwiches, camping bits and bobs, fishing tackle, OS maps, lottery tickets and much more.

Glen Loin runs between the Arrochar Alps to the west and Cruach Tairbeirt (415m/1361') to the east. A signposted walk begins opposite the Village Shop with an information board detailing the route. It is possible to follow this path to remote Glen Sloy, from where Loch Sloy feeds the Inveruglas power station, or to follow Inveruglas Water down to Loch Lomond. The woodlands in Glen Loin are a Site of Special Scientific Interest and home to red and roe deer, red squirrels and foxes. Golden eagles and sparrowhawks can also sometimes be spotted. In the Glen Loin caves, Robert the Bruce allegedly took refuge after a defeat. Later, the caves were used by cattle rustlers on the Glen Loin drove route.

The Loch Long Hotel was once a temperance establishment called Henderson's Hotel. It is now owned by holiday company Lochs and Glens and enjoys views overlooking the water.

Glenloin Caravan & Camping Site is a large, welcoming site just across the road from the loch with an excellent on-site take-away.

The Kitchen Garden, next to the filling station, sells hot and cold drinks and a large selection of reasonably priced, freshly made rolls – including some with haggis! Open all year.

Mactavish's Filling Station sells a variety of goods as well as fuel and calor gas.

Lochside Walk: From the large National Park car park (pay and display) a path follows the head of the loch amongst oak, willow, rowan and silver birch and meadowsweet across a small footbridge over the River Loin. Along the way interesting carved figures tell of the Vikings and later visitors to the area, famous people who have passed this way and wildlife to look out for. Picnic tables by the water provide a chance to spot oystercatchers, curlews and other waders searching for food in the shallow water near the shore.

Carved Figures by Loch Long

Arrochar To Inveraray

From Arrochar, the A83 snakes round the end of Loch Long, following the old military road beneath the towering peaks of the Arrochar Alps before climbing through Glen Croe up to well named Rest And Be Thankful. From there, the A83 continues through Glen Kinglas to meet Loch Fyne and then on to Inveraray. Meanwhile the B828 branches off from Rest and Be Thankful through Gleann Mor to Lochgoilhead, passing the southern entrance to Gleann Beag, more commonly known as "Hell's Glen." (See page 40.)

Forest Walks: Just west of Arrochar, the Forestry Commission car park and visitor centre is a popular starting point for The Arrochar Alps, in particular for the ascent of The Cobbler.

Ardgartan Forest, on the western shore of Loch Long, is managed by the Forestry Commission. The upper reaches are known as The Bowling Green. The main peaks include The Saddle (521m/1709') and Cnoc Coinnich (761m/2496'). The forest is criss-crossed with many tracks and cycle paths and is popular for outdoor training, commandos from as far away as Norway coming to experience the rugged terrain.

Outdoor Training in Ardgartan Forest

Ardgartan Camping Site

Ardgartan Caravan & Camping Site offers activities to both residents and visitors, including gorge walking, archery and cycle hire. The well stocked shop sells a wide range of necessities, local produce and superb coffee! The site is also popular with deer who come down from the hills on most nights.

Ardgartan Visitor Centre (seasonal) has picnic tables, an information centre and access to the forest tracks, including The Cowal Way. In the car park are some wood sculptures of eagles and otters. 3 km/2 miles south of the visitor centre, along a loch-side track, is Coilessan where a ruined mill remains. For the less energetic, The Ardgartan Peninsula Circuit (2 km/1.3 miles) provides a gentler stroll or cycle ride.

Glen Croe was the main droving route from the west, later becoming a military road. The "modern" trunk road was completed in 1941 and is very dramatic with high mountains to either side, towering above the depths of the glen with much evidence of rock falls. Huge wire mesh shields protect the road. The lower slopes are covered with a mix of lichen-covered deciduous trees and conifers with many burns rushing down to join Croe Water on its way to Loch Long. The glen is particularly atmospheric on days when the mist appears to hang from the trees. The stiff gradiant of the road is a popular challenge for cyclists.

Glen Croe from Rest & Be Thankful

The Honeymoon Bridge, 4.8 km/3 miles west of Arrochar, is named after a 1950s tragedy. A young married couple, separated for four years by the husband's job, set out to enjoy a second honeymoon but vanished. Several days later the car was discovered to have veered off the road into the river, killing both occupants.

Rest And Be Thankful, at 246m/860', is the highest point on the A83 between Glen Croe and Glen Kinglas. It was named by soldiers who built the military road in the mid 18th century and who inscribed the words on a stone. It is easy to imagine how thankful travellers and their beasts would be to reach this point! A replacement stone, though difficult to read now, stands near the car park.

This is the popular departure point for the ascent of Beinn an Lochain (901m/2955'), Ben Dornich (847m/2778') The Brack (787m/2581') and Beinn Luibhean (858m/2814'). On a clear day the views are spectacular – up to the Cobbler (Ben Arthur) and down to the old drove route winding its way along the floor of Glen Croe.

From Rest & Be Thankful, the A83 continues through Glen Kinglas to be joined by the A815 before it sweeps round the head of Loch Fyne to Inveraray. Nestling between the two main roads are Cairndow and Ardkinglas, a delightful detour.

Ardkinglas and Cairndow

Ardkinglass House

Ardkinglas: The Ardkinglas Estate was Campbell territory from 1396 but in the 19th century passed, through marriage, to the Callendars of Craigforth. In the early 20th century it was purchased by the Nobles. It is a good example of a surviving "designed landscape" including gardens, woodland, an ornamental lake and parkland.

Ardkinglas House is magnificent. Completed in 1907 for Sir Andrew Noble, it was designed by Lorimer, one of Scotland's most renowned architects who also designed the National War Memorial at Edinburgh Castle. Ardkinglas is built in the Scottish Arts & Crafts style and is a "mecca" for present day architects. Especially noteworthy is the plasterwork, oak panelling, internal stonework and a lovely fountain adjacent to the house. At the centre of a small pond a mermaid holds a fish, water spouting from its mouth. House tours: Fridays. Apr.- Oct. Booking essential. Tel: 01499 600261

Ardkinglas Woodland Gardens are delightful. Stroll along well maintained paths amongst some of Britain's tallest fir trees and beautiful flowering shrubs. An excellent leaflet (available from a dispenser near the entrance) details what is to be seen. Woodland picnic area. Dogs on leads welcome. Open all year, dawn to dusk.

Cairndow is pronounced "Cairndoo" from the Gaelic "cairn dhu", meaning "black rock", although the parish and its church go by the older name of Kilmorich after an early saint.

Kilmorich Church

Kilmorich Church is a beautiful octagonal, church built in 1816, the date proclaimed in Roman numerals MDCCCXVI. Inside is a beautiful baptismal roll and the family trees of the Campbells, Livingstones, Erskines and Callanders of Ardkinglas. The muted pastel colours of the interior create an aura of peace. Outside stand ancient gravestones. Open daily.

Cairndow Stagecoach Inn

Cairndow Stagecoach Inn was a coaching inn. The Stables Restaurant occupies the converted stables. Famous visitors included Boswell and Johnson on their 1773 tour of The Highlands and, in 1816, Dorothy and William Wordsworth. The beer garden on the loch shore must surely be one of Scotland's most scenic. Run by the same family for the last forty years, the inn is open all year, serving food from midday to 21.00. Live music during the season.

War Memorial: By the junction with the main road a simple Celtic cross overlooks the loch.

The Head of Loch Fyne

Loch Fyne is the longest of Scotland's sea lochs and has always been important for herring fishing. Smoked herring became the now-famous Loch Fyne kippers. Today, fish farms harvesting oysters, mussels and salmon are a major part of the local economy, along with tourism.

Steep sided Glen Fyne carries the River Fyne to the northern end of the loch, swelled by many tributaries from either side. A private track follows the river

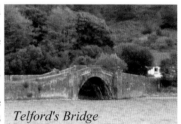
Telford's Bridge

some 10 km/6.2 miles to Lochan Larige Reservoir and beyond. There are several waterfalls along this stretch of river. The A83 sweeps round the head of the loch.

Telford's Bridge: To the right of the A83 bridge over the River Fyne is the original Telford bridge.

Walkers' Car Park: At the head of the loch is a car park for those wanting to explore Glen Fyne.

Fyne Ales is an award-winning craft brewery, established in 2001 in the converted milking parlour of Achadunan Farm. There is a brewery shop and a café serving beef pies. Near the car park live a herd of highland cattle who are fed on the spent grain from the brewery.

Fyne Ales

Loch Fyne Oyster Bar, once a simple roadside stall, is now a popular and sophisticated seafood restaurant, willing to serve a single oyster for anyone wishing to try this delicacy for the first time! Open daily.

Loch Fyne Deli sell the very best of Scottish produce; seafood, meat & dairy products, ready prepared meals, home-made cakes, jams & preserves.

Fyne Oysters

Weather Information: Next to the oyster bar a board gives up-to-date details about weather, tides etc.

The Tree Shop sells plants, books, cards, gifts, wild bird food and much more. There is also a café here.

"Here We Are" has local information and a fascinating exhibition about the history of the local community. An aquarium shows creatures which live in Loch Fyne and a set of labelled logs show the different trees which grow in Ardkinglas Forest. Nearby are an ancient graveyard and signposted walks.

Loch Fyne Deli

Dunderave Castle stands on a promontory midway between the head of the loch and Inveraray. The castle was built in 1596 for the MacNaughton chief but forfeited to the Campbells a century later because of a broken marriage contract. Author Neil Munro (1863 – 1930) used the castle as the basis for his novel "Castle of Doom". The castle was extensively restored in the early 20th century by architect Robert Lorimer for the Noble family and is still occupied.

The Tree Shop

Inveraray

The original fishing settlement, a royal burgh since 1648, was demolished by The Duke of Argyll when he built the present Inveraray Castle. The town is a charming 18th century "planned" town, the first in Scotland, built to re-house the displaced fishermen and provide a pier for landing herring.

Inveraray has an attractive front and a wide main street dominated by the parish church at its head. It is a popular and bustling place with a variety of shops, hotels and restaurants and a perfectly preserved 19th century jail.

Inveraray Bridge nestles below Dun Corr Bhile and carries the A83 over the River Aray, replacing an earlier bridge which was swept away in 1722. The present elegant, two arched one was built in 1776 to a design by Robert Mylne, as was much of the town, along with designs by John Adam.

Inveraray Castle

Inveraray Castle was built by the 3rd Duke of Argyll in the mid 18th century replacing an earlier one destroyed in 1644. It was initially designed by Vanbrugh and developed by Morris and Adam as the main seat of Clan Campbell. The approach is a magnificent tree-lined drive, the borders laid out in the shape of the Scottish flag. The gardens are renowned for rhododendrons which are ideally suited to the climate here. Open daily Apr. – Oct. 10.00. – 17.45. Gift shop & tea room serving teas, coffees and home baking. Dun na Cuaiche, to the north of the town and overlooking the castle, has a lookout tower at its summit. It is accessible via a steep woodland climb with stunning views over Loch Fyne.

The Argyll Hotel is an impressive hotel on the front, designed by John Adam and built in 1755 as The Great Inn. Boswell and Johnson stayed here, as later did the Wordsworths and Robert Burns. It was also where visiting judges stayed, reputedly with a "cellar" of their own!

Visit Scotland occupies an imposing building on the front, originally the 1757 courthouse and prison which was replaced by the larger, more secure, building at the top of the town. Visit Scotland offers information, an accommodation booking service and a range of books, maps and gifts for sale.

Cross Green is the grassed area in front of the War Memorial. Cattle markets were held here until the mid 20th century.

Inveraray War Memorial, on Cross Green, features a fine bronze statue by William Kellock Brown of a kilted soldier of The Argyll and Sutherland Highlanders looking out over the loch.

The Pier was originally built in 1759 but extended as the herring fleet became larger and steamers began to arrive. Until the 1960s a ferry crossed the loch to St. Catherine's.

Inveraray Maritime Museum

Inveraray Maritime Museum features two Clyde "puffers" - Eilean Easdale and The Vital Spark, of Parahandy fame from the novels of Neil Munro who was born in Inveraray in 1863. Arctic

Penguin, one of the last surviving iron sailing ships, houses various maritime exhibitions.

The Pier Shop sells teas and coffees, hot & cold snacks, ice cream, Scottish tablet, gifts and newspapers.

Iona Cross: At the end of the main street stands an Iona Memorial Cross, one of very few seen on the mainland.

Main Street:

As well as banks, pharmacies etc. there are outdoor and gift shops and a number of nice places to eat, several with pavement tables. Shops and cafés are too numerous to mention individually. The following is just a selection.

Main Street, Inveraray

MacIntyres, established in 1863, sell a wide selection of tweeds and tartans, knitwear and quality Scottish gifts.

The House of Scotland sell a large variety of Scottish souvenirs.

David's Bakery sells ice cream, home-made soup and wonderfully large slabs of cake (complete with take-away fork if required.) The Victoria sponge is really yummy!

The Royal Borough Café: Pavement seating, home-made ice cream, wine list.

Highland Arts sell quality Scottish gifts.

Brambles: A really interesting and extensive menu, home-baking, sit in or out.

Loch Fyne Whiskies is a "must visit" for all lovers of the amber nectar. The range includes many rare whiskies, a special Loch Fyne blended whisky and the truly magnificent Loch Fyne Whisky Liqueur – a luxurious mix of twelve year old whisky, chocolate, tangerine & orange. Mmmm!

The George Hotel was originally built in 1770 as two houses in the new town. Six years later the ground floor of each was made into a temporary church to accommodate Gaelic and English speakers respectively, prior to the building of the present church. The two houses were amalgamated to become a hotel in 1860 by the Clark family who, seven generations on, still own and run the hotel which has won several awards for its restaurant and bar. Full menu served all day

Church Square:

Inveraray Parish Church, completed in 1805, is a classical style building dominating the main street. The church interior was divided by a central wall to provide separate accommodation for English and Gaelic speaking congregations. Open daily in summer. Winter - Sun. and Wed.

The Drinking Fountain at the top of Main Street was gifted in 1893 by the Rev. Neil Macpherson, minister of the parish.

Drinking Fountain

Inveraray Jail: Inveraray was the principal centre of administration and justice for a large area, with its court and jail built in 1820. The jail closed in 1889 but has been restored and is a major visitor attraction, giving a fascinating insight into justice and punishment in days gone by. Fascinating audio visual effects enable visitors to sit in on a trial. Open all year.

The Cottage Restaurant, down a small alley at the top of Main Street, has an extremely reasonably priced menu of good wholesome food.

The Stable Gallery, tucked away at the top of the main street, is a real gem with original art by Scottish artists and a range of unusual prints, cards and gifts including mugs printed with Scottish art. Whilst in the gallery be sure to look up at the unusual mural on the gable end.

The Avenue:

The Bell Tower was built by the 10th Duke of Argyll in memory of Clan Campbell members killed during WWI. It is 37.8m/126' high and contains ten bells, weighing almost eight tons, the second heaviest set of bells in the World. Inside are exhibitions on The Great War and campanology (bell ringing). The view from the top of the hundred and seventy-seven steps is magnificent. Open. Weekdays 10.30 - 16.30 Jul. - Sep.

The Bell Tower

The Wishing Well, above the town off the A819, is a classical style well-house built into the hillside over a natural spring. It was designed by William Adam and erected in 1747. At one time water was piped from here down to the town.

Inveraray Woollen Mill sells knitwear, tartan, Scottish gifts and whiskies. Upstairs is The Anvil Coffee Shop.

The Avenue Car Park is on the site of an avenue of beech trees planted in the 17th century by the 8th and 9th Earls of Argyll in response to a Scottish Government bill urging landowners to plant trees. The trees stood until the 1950s but became dangerous. New young trees have now been planted.

All Saints Church is an attractive, red granite church, designed by Wardrop and Anderson in the Gothic style and built in 1885. Open daily Apr. – Sep.

Inveraray Golf Club, 0.8 km/0.5 miles south of the town, is a nine hole course. Golfers can be forgiven for being distracted by the magnificent views of the loch! Visitors welcome.

The Loch Fyne Hotel offers luxurious accommodation, loch views, excellent bistro or formal dining and the chance to indulge at the leisure club or on-site spa.

The First House Hotel is a lovely lochside Georgian turreted building, so named because it was the first house to be built (1753) in the new town.

MotoScotland.com, Scotland's first and only off road motorcycle training centre, provides an amazing experience - professional skills tuition and trail riding amongst 50,000 acres of stunning scenery. Motorbike tours and hire also available. For details Tel: 01499 320460. Mob: 07900 575899. www.motoscotland.com

Taxi: James Campbell Private Hire. 01499 500277

6. LOCHGOILHEAD, CARRICK & HELL'S GLEN

From Rest And Be Thankful the torturous B828 winds dramatically into Gleann Mor and on to the remote and picturesque Lochgoilhead. Dominated to the south by towering Ben Donich (847m/2778'), this single track road is not for the faint-hearted but a beautiful drive whatever the season. Conifers interspersed with deciduous trees, including silver birch and rowan, produce a patchwork of many shades of green. There are several places with access into the forest and deer can often be glimpsed. From the junction with the B839 Hell's Glen Road the road south follows the River Goil. The stone walls here are particularly picturesque – heavily covered in different mosses and lichen. Several walking and mountain bike trails lead into the forest.

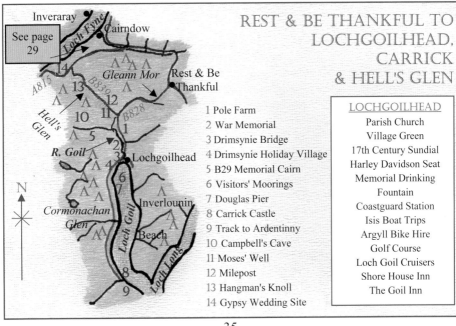

REST & BE THANKFUL TO LOCHGOILHEAD, CARRICK & HELL'S GLEN

1 Pole Farm
2 War Memorial
3 Drimsynie Bridge
4 Drimsynie Holiday Village
5 B29 Memorial Cairn
6 Visitors' Moorings
7 Douglas Pier
8 Carrick Castle
9 Track to Ardentinny
10 Campbell's Cave
11 Moses' Well
12 Milepost
13 Hangman's Knoll
14 Gypsy Wedding Site

LOCHGOILHEAD
Parish Church
Village Green
17th Century Sundial
Harley Davidson Seat
Memorial Drinking Fountain
Coastguard Station
Isis Boat Trips
Argyll Bike Hire
Golf Course
Loch Goil Cruisers
Shore House Inn
The Goil Inn

Pole Farm (privately owned) in the bottom of the glen is very typical of 18th century farms in this area, built around a courtyard. Sheep farming was dominant when the farm, now a listed building, was erected. A "smearing shed" remains – before modern chemicals, sheep were smeered with a greasy substance to protect them from diseases spread by insects. Much of the area was later cleared of sheep in favour of forestry.

Conifers make this area a favourite haunt of red squirrels – note the unusual road sign where the road crosses the River Goil. A little further on, a minor road branches off to Drimsynie and Carrick Castle. (See pages 38 & 39)

War Memorial: At the junction is a simple, elegant Celtic cross, the pine forest behind forming a backdrop.

Lochgoilhead

(Gaelic: Ceann Loch Goighle) The B839 ends at this charming village with its row of pretty white terraced cottages. Dominated by Beinn Bheula (779m/2555') to the south west, it feels remote but is well served by local amenities. A welcoming atmosphere makes the detour worthwhile. The village was once part of the Campbells' Ardkinglas Estate. Major development occurred when steamers began to ply up and down the Clyde Estuary,

Lochgoilhead

transporting mail, people and goods and considerably shortening the journey time between Inveraray and Oban. Lochgoilhead Pier was one of the earliest on the Clyde and The Loch Goil and Loch Long Steam Packet Co. one of the first such companies, established about 1825. Passengers alighted at Lochgoilhead to travel by stagecoach to St. Catherines, this route having been only a grass track until 1820 when the road was built by the Laird of Ardkinglas and Campbell of Drimsynie. By the 1840s a regular steamer service was operating. Some of the larger houses date from this time, built as holiday homes by wealthy Clyde businessmen. Entire families, including servants, would spend the summer here, the men commuting daily down the Clyde. It is said that as much business was carried on over the silver service on the steamer as in the offices of Glasgow. The Loch Goil & Loch Long Steam Packet Co. operated until 1909.

The Car Park in the village centre has attractive hanging baskets topped with ships and whales and a wrought iron seat with a steamer worked into its design. Nearby, picnic tables enjoy picturesque views down the loch.

Lochgoilhead Parish Church is also known as The Church Of The Three Holy Brethren, thought to be early Irish missionary saints. It is an imposing white-painted building with medieval origins although the present building dates mainly from the 18th century. The wooden pulpit, thought to date from 1791, was brought here in 1955 from another church. The simple font of unknown date and origin is hewn from a block of sandstone. Open daily.

The Village Green is a grassed area at the head of the loch, accessed via a series of wrought iron gates. Beneath an ancient sycamore tree are the remains of a water pump and stone trough. The wrought iron seats reflect the area, featuring bats and dolphins. Nearby stands a carved otter.

Obelisk Sundial

Sundial: Visible from the green is a 17th century obelisk sundial, a wedding present to Sir Colin Campbell, the 8th Laird of Ardkinglas.

The Shore House Inn

The Shore House Inn enjoys a superb location at the head of the loch and offers accommodation as well as a cosy bar and a light and airy restaurant with a full menu. It is especially renowned for pizzas from its wood burning pizza oven, one of only a handful in the country. Open 12.00 – 23.00 Wed. – Sun. except Jan/Feb. Live music every Friday.

The Goil Inn, formerly The Lochgoilhead Hotel, was a coaching inn and has lovely oak panelling in the bar, where there is a model of The Waverley, made for the hotel in 1984 by David Logan. Open daily for lunches and dinner, with a take-away service from 17.00.

Harley Davidson Carved Seat: At the junction near the hotel is a seat in the shape of the Harley Davidson logo, crafted by Graham Jones from the remains of a local tree and gifted to the village by the Clyde Valley Harley Davidson Group.

Memorial Drinking Fountain: Also at the junction, this was erected "by voluntary subscription to the late Mr. Neil Campbell" who

Harley Davidson Seat

was the postmaster at Lochgoilhead from 1882 until just before the turn of the century.

The Post Office is a regular "Aladdin's Cave", selling groceries, newspapers, confectionary, ice cream, postcards, fresh fruit & vegetables, bread and many other necessities including cappuccino coffee. Outside is an interesting information board about the area.

Drinking Fountain

D M Automarine offer full garage and repair facilities, self drive boats for day or half-day bookings and fishing tackle for sale or hire with boats. Boat hire: Apr. – Oct. Tel: 01301 703 432. Mob: 07776 185514.

Boat Hire on Loch Goil

Public toilets are on a small lane opposite The Goil Inn.

Visitors' Moorings, of which there are ten, are yellow and marked "visitor".

The Coastguard Station is situated by the slipway at the end of the main street.

Isis Skippered Boat Charter is a relaxing way to see seals and other wildlife at close quarters with an experienced and knowledgeable local skipper. On-board toilet, evening wine & dine cruises available. (Seasonal) Tel: 0779 6555206

Inverlounin: The public road ends by the coastguard station but it is possible to continue on foot to the waterfalls at Inverlounin. Inverlounin House, now elegant self catering accommodation, was built in 1876 by a Glasgow businessman. 2 km/1.2miles further along the shoreline is Beach, so named after a legendary monster (Beoch) said to inhabit the loch. The shore is now home to less terrifying creatures - seals! The track here forms part of the 15 km/9.3 miles walk/cycle route around the end of the peninsula to Ardgartan.

B29 Memorial Cairn: On the slopes of Stob na Boine Druim-fhinn, north west of Lochgoilhead, is a memorial to the crew of a B29 Superfortress bomber. The aircraft crashed here in poor weather in January 1949, killing all its American crew who were going home on leave after participating in The Berlin Airlift. Mystery surrounds the crash - rumours of a consignment of diamonds on board were never proved. Members of the local Air Cadets built the cairn.

The Western Shore of Loch Goil

The 8 km/5 mile minor road between the B839 and Carrick Castle was built in 1953 when electricity arrived in the area. Prior to this, a generator at the garage was used to charge 12V household batteries, although most households still used paraffin lamps for lighting.

Drimsynie Holiday Village is a holiday caravan and chalet village incorporating an excellent swimming pool and leisure centre with sauna and jacuzzi which is open to non residents. Activities include indoor bowling, snooker, ice skating, archery, water walking and body zorbing.

Drimsynie Bridge & Holiday Village

Drimsynie Bridge: As the road rounds the head of the loch through the holiday village and crosses the river, a lovely 19th century two arched bridge can be seen upstream. It carried the road until the mid 20th century.

The Drimsynie House Hotel is an imposing castellated mansion at the heart of the holiday village. The corner turrets hide the chimneys. Completed in 1860, the house was built for the Neilson family on the site of an earlier house at the mouth of a ravine formed by the Eas a Chruisgein. It retains many original features, including plasterwork. Today it offers comfortable loch-view accommodation and a range of dining options.

Argyll Bike Hire, adjacent to the hotel, has a choice of bikes, including children's, for hire and which can be delivered by arrangement. Tel: 01301 703177 Mob: 07771 844786.

Drimsynie Golf Course is exceptionally scenic, having nine holes right at the head of the loch. Club hire available from reception.

Convenience Store: In the grounds of the holiday village a well stocked shop sells groceries, wines & spirits, phone cards, souvenirs etc. Open daily 08.00 – 20.00. (Shorter hours in winter.)

As the road climbs away from Drimsynie, there are panoramic views down the loch and back towards Lochgoilhead, nestling beneath Ben Donich. The two shores contrast greatly, for the far side is dominated by a MOD installation, a naval base having existed here since WWII and now used for warship trials.

Ardroy Outdoor Education Centre offers residential courses for groups.

Loch Goil Cruisers, at Douglas Pier, offer motorboat hire for those wishing to enjoy the scenery and wildlife from the water or to try their hand at fishing. (Tackle hire available). Tel: 01301 703382. Mob: 0778 7516709

Douglas Pier. Steamers delivered mail here for communities on western Loch Goil before continuing to Lochgoilhead. At one time Douglas Pier had its own post office.

The Lodge: 2.5 km/1.8 miles south of Drimsynie is The Lodge, a lovely house dating from 1863 with later additions by renowned architect William Leiper who was known for his Gothic Revival style. The house installed a hydro power wheel for generating electricity during the 1920s and 1930s which can still be used if needed.

Cormonachan Glen: 2.5 km/1.8 miles south of Douglas Pier the Cormonachan Burn rushes down in a series of spectacular waterfalls before plunging under the road to the loch. A popular walk is up the glen to the ruins of the abandoned 17th century village of Upper Cormonachan.

Carrick Castle, jutting out into the loch, is an imposing sight. An earlier castle probably existed  *Carrick Castle* here but the present ruins are thought to date from the 13th century. Originally a Lamont fortification, it fell into the hands of the Campbells during the 14th century. In the 17th century, it was burned as reprisal against the Campbells for supporting the Duke of Monmouth's rebellion against James VII. Now privately owned, there is no public access.

Picnic area: By the castle are a free car park and a pleasant picnic area.

Carrick Pier, adjacent to the castle, was in use from 1877 until 1945 and then rebuilt by the military in the mid 1950s. In its heyday, a steamer would stop here daily to deliver mail.

Ardentinny walk: The public road ends at the castle but a track continues to the farm then on to Ardentinny, a walk of approximately two and a half hours.

The B839 runs the length of Hell's Glen (Gleann Beag), linking the B828 from Rest And Be Thankful with the A815 along the north eastern shore of Loch Fyne. Scenic in either direction, travelling south to north the route emerges high above Loch Fyne with birds' eye views over the loch to Inveraray and beyond. From the B828 junction the road twists between the peaks of Stob an Eas (732m/2401') to the right and Cruach nam Mult (611m/2004') on the left. This was once the main route from Lowland Scotland to Inveraray. Until the early 20th century horse drawn carriages traversed this route twice daily from Dunoon. Several theories exist for the name "Hell's Glen": One is the challenge presented by the road in bad weather; another refers to the smoke and flames which once emitted from the glen's open air charcoal smelters and a third, more sinister, is that the glen was named for the condemned prisoners from Inveraray Jail, brought here to be hanged – the belief being that ghosts cannot cross water! There are many caves in the area and evidence of early Bronze Age settlers as well as the ruins of later black houses.

Moses' Well: 1.5 km/0.9 miles from the southern end of the glen is a large wayside stone where water spouts from a lion's head. One story is that the well was constructed in the 19th century by a minister and named after the biblical tale in which Moses caused water to spout from a rock. The well was actually instigated by Hugh Cameron, a coachman who paid for the well as a watering place for his horses. The water was thought to have supernatural powers: Legend tells of its healing properties and, allegedly, gypsies washed their crystal balls here. An information board provides insights into the history of the glen.

Moses' Well

Campbells' Cave can be found on the hill above Moses' Well.

Mile Posts in Hell's Glen are picturesque cast iron structures with a pointing hand to indicate direction. Such markers were compulsory from 1767. They were not only informative for travellers but also used to work out charges for hired horses.

Hangman's Knoll: The road winds up through the forest to suddenly emerge high over Loch Fyne with spectacular views to Inveraray to the left and Dunderave Castle far below. At this point, known as Hangman's Knoll, was a gallows where prisoners from Inveraray Jail were hanged.

The road then drops steeply to meet the A815 Glen Kinglas to Dunoon road.

Gipsy Weddings traditionally occurred at this junction, the place marked by a heart of white stones set into the road surface. When this part of the road was bypassed in the 1970s the heart and its surrounds were incorporated into a nearby field.

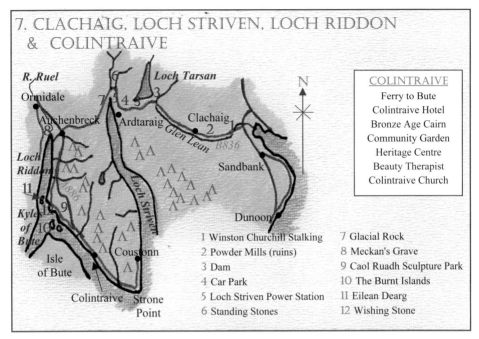

R. Ruel
Ormidale
Loch Tarsan
N
Auchenbreck
Ardtaraig
Clachaig
Glen Lean
B836
Sandbank
Loch Riddon
Kyle of Bute
Coustonn
Dunoon
Isle of Bute
Colintraive Strone Point

COLINTRAIVE

Ferry to Bute
Colintraive Hotel
Bronze Age Cairn
Community Garden
Heritage Centre
Beauty Therapist
Colintraive Church

1 Winston Churchill Stalking	7 Glacial Rock
2 Powder Mills (ruins)	8 Meckan's Grave
3 Dam	9 Caol Ruadh Sculpture Park
4 Car Park	10 The Burnt Islands
5 Loch Striven Power Station	11 Eilean Dearg
6 Standing Stones	12 Wishing Stone

North of Dunoon the B836 branches westwards across the Cowal Peninsula to some of its most remote and haunting places.

Winston Churchill Stalking at Balagowan is a family run business. A purpose-built venison larder stocks various cuts, venison burgers, venison and pheasant sausages etc. To arrange deer stalking Tel: 01369 705319.

Clachaig is a pretty hamlet of cottages built for workers at the powder mills which once filled this part of Glean Lean. Established in 1838, the works were extended during the Crimean War (1853 – 1856). Raw materials were imported through Sandbank where barrels for storing the gunpowder were made. Twenty years later the works closed but re-opened in 1891 for ten years. Remains of the buildings have now largely disappeared amongst woodland.

Glean Lean: ("The Broad Glen") The single track road winds its way alongside The Little Eachaig River between rowan, bracken and Forestry Commission plantations, making it a popular habitat for red squirrels.

Loch Tarsan (Gaelic: Loch Stroigheann) is a reservoir for the hydro-electric system, bounded by a small earth dam at the head of Glean Lean and a much larger one in Glen Tarsan. The loch is stocked with brown trout for fishing. Permits available from Campbells, Dunoon. Tel: 01369 704191.

From Loch Tarsan the road drops to the head of Loch Striven. Opposite a car park on the right is a

Loch Tarsan

track to the loch shore. The pipe running down the hill opposite is evidence of the hydro-electric scheme.

The Head of Loch Striven

Loch Striven Power Station is small, built to house a single turbine. It is not unattractive, having been designed by architect Reginald Fairlie to resemble a church.

Gleann Laolgh, at the head of Loch Striven, is the site of some standing stones, about 500m/0.3 miles from the road. (Private track, no vehicles.) The track continues into the forest to the head of the glen.

Glacial Rock: As the road rounds the head of Loch Striven a huge roadside boulder is beautifully marked with striation scars - deep scratches caused by glacial upheaval.

The road then turns south along the opposite shore with spectacular views down the loch before dropping to join the A886. To the north is Glen Daruel (see page 44) and to the south is Colintraive and Strone Point, separated from the Isle of Bute by the eastern Kyles of Bute. (In Scotland "Kyle" denotes a narrow stretch of water separating two islands or an island from the mainland.)

Auchenbreck was once the site of the castle of Sir Duncan Campbell whose descendants supported the Jacobite cause. A mill and the present farmhouse were built of stone taken from the castle, all of which remains is a flat area where it once stood.

Loch Riddon (also called Loch Ruel) at the head of the Kyles of Bute is popular with yachts. Just under 3 km/2 miles south of Auchenbrek the B866 branches off to the right to rejoin the main road some 4 km/2.5 miles further on. This detour is spectacularly beautiful, especially in the opposite direction so we recommend you return this way. (See page 43.)

Colintraive

Colintraive, separated from The Isle of Bute by only 300m/ 333 yards, is one of those special places; remote, beautiful and welcoming. Its name derives from the Gaelic for "swimming straits" – here cattle were swum across from Bute. However, Colintraive was another community subjected to the 18th century Clearances when sheep grazing proved more profitable than tenanted farming. Today, the village is a popular yachting destination.

Colintraive Ferry makes one of the shortest of all Scotland's ferry crossings, the journey to Rhubodach on Bute taking only a few minutes. A ferry is known to have existed here since at least 1865.

The Colintraive Hotel was built in 1850 as a hunting lodge for The Marquis of Bute. Sympathetically restored, it retains all its original character with an unusual spiral staircase. It is a stunning hotel with a warm welcome for everyone (including angelic children

The Colintraive Hotel

and dogs with well behaved owners!) The menu is wonderful – fresh local produce, a wide choice of seafood, home-made puddings and a children's menu of real food. Allergies catered for. Visitors' moorings available and a sailors' shower room. Open all year. Tel: 01700 841207

Colintraive Village Post Office, like Dr. Who's Tardis, seems larger inside than out! Groceries, fresh bread, wines & spirits, newspapers, milk, hand-made gifts, home-made Scottish tablet and a local cookery book. Cash available. (Hereabouts cash machines are few and far between: It is always possible to obtain cash from a post office.)

Bronze Age Cairn: Opposite the hotel can be seen a mound, the site of a bronze age cairn.

Community Garden: This is a tranquil place with seats and tables (including a Wendy house and mini picnic area for children), a barbecue, waterfall, a beautiful carved thistle and lots of wildlife – look out for red squirrels. The pond was once the millpond for a meal mill which stood where the village hall now stands.

The Heritage Centre is a lively exhibition about village life over the past 150 years, including old farming implements, a Ferguson tractor, a Royal Mail bicycle, traditional desks and collections of old letters and textbooks. Activity sheets for children make this a good wet day visit! Admission free. Open daily May – Sept.

Holly Walker Beauty Therapist: For holiday pampering – facials, manicures, waxing, pedicures etc. in comfortable surroundings. Tel: 01700 841301

Colintraive Church was built in 1840 with funds raised by Mrs. Janet Campbell, the laird's wife. Inside is a marble memorial to her. Another plaque remembers the Reverend Alex MacGilp who was the minister for forty-five years from 1886. Each pew has a door with an umbrella stand. Two stained glass windows commemorate those who fell in the two World Wars.

Colintraive Church

Strone Point

This is where the eastern Kyles of Bute joins Loch Striven, is 5 km/ 3 miles beyond Colintraive. The narrow road clings to the shore line, somewhat precariously in places! (A good place for blackberries in season.) There are excellent views of Bute to the south and the Toward Peninsula to the east. Strone Point has a nice shingle beach. The road peters out at Coustonn some 2 km/1.2miles further on.

Loch Riddon Minor Road: From Colintraive, north, the B866 leaves the main road to rejoin it 4 km/2.5 miles further on. It runs along the lochside amongst ancient woodland with beautiful gnarled oak trees. Herons can often be seen fishing in the loch here.

Caol Ruadh Sculpture Park is an outdoor sculpture gallery in the grounds of a former Victorian mansion, providing a wonderful backdrop to many sculptures, including Rob Mulholland's atmospheric group of stainless steel figures which stand in the water catching the reflections. Another sculpture, "Ebb and Flow" by Kevin Dagg, is a small croft house which appears and disappears with the tide and whose roof seems to be floating away. Closed in winter.

Caol Ruadh
Sculpture Park

The Burnt Islands are so named because of the vitrified fort which was discovered on Eilean Buidh. (A vitrified fort was built of dry stone and then subjected to intense heat, fusing the stones together.)

Eilean Dearg, the island in the middle of the loch, was the site of a Campbell castle. It is also known as One Tree Island as a solitary tree once stood here. Thought to be secure, the castle was used to store gunpowder. However, government troops raided the island, set fire to the gunpowder and the entire castle was blown into the loch.

The Wishing Stone is a large, oddly shaped stone between the road and the sea, south of Port an Eilein. Bow three times towards Eilean Dearg before making your wish and it may be granted!

8. GLENDARUEL & CAOL GHLEANN

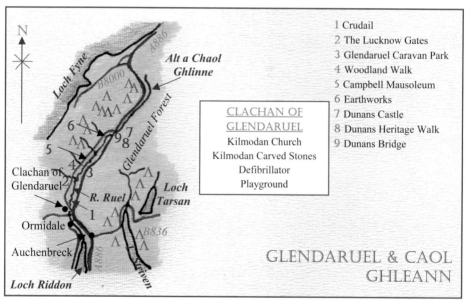

1 Crudail
2 The Lucknow Gates
3 Glendaruel Caravan Park
4 Woodland Walk
5 Campbell Mausoleum
6 Earthworks
7 Dunans Castle
8 Dunans Heritage Walk
9 Dunans Bridge

CLACHAN OF
GLENDARUEL
Kilmodan Church
Kilmodan Carved Stones
Defibrillator
Playground

GLENDARUEL & CAOL
GHLEANN

Glendaruel means "Glen of the red", possibly after an 11th century battle: Norse invaders were slaughtered here and the river was said to run red with blood. An alternative explanation could be the local red soil. The River Ruel flows into Loch Riddon (also called Loch Ruel) near Auchenbreck. From here the A886 north follows the edge of the Glendaruel Forest on the eastern side of the glen to eventually emerge on the shores of Loch Fyne. However, a far more interesting route, signposted Clachan of Glendaruel, follows the old road up the western side of the glen. (A clachan is a hamlet.) In summer, the lower glen is a sea of colour with cornflowers, meadowsweet and many species of fern growing in the forks of trees. The damp conditions also provide an ideal habitat for alder trees with their miniature cones.

Clachan of Glendaruel & Glendaruel West

Kilmodan Church

Kilmodan Church & Carved Stones: This beautiful 18th century church is on the site of two earlier churches and dedicated to St. Modan, one of two early saints of that name who travelled widely through Scotland. Inside, centuries and generations seem to overlap. The church has three wooden galleries, with separate staircases and external doors – in order that estranged branches of the Campbell family need not meet! Not unusually for this type of church, the bell pull is outside. The high pulpit is typical of the era. A collection of early photographs shows previous ministers, one of the earliest holding office from 1837 to 1843. A memorial commemorates the Maclaurins – The Rev. John Maclaurin was minister at Kilmodan after the 1688 revolution. His son, also John, was instrumental in the building of Glasgow's first mental hospital which later became The Royal Asylum. One of his sons became a famous mathematician and friend of Isaac Newton. Outside is a small stone building, cared for by Historic Scotland, housing ten large 14th and 15th century grave slabs, carved with men in armour and mythical creatures by itinerant carvers who travelled the countryside executing such work.

Ancient Grave Slab

Defibrillator: Near the red post box at Clachan of Glendaruel is a defibrillator.

Playground: Along the minor road a pretty, double arched, stone bridge crosses the river near a children's playground.

Battle of Crudail: The flat area immediately to the east of the stone bridge is known as Crudail. During the 11th century a fierce battle took place here between the Norweigans and the Scots. Meckan, son of King Magnus of Norway, was slain. A plaque marks his grave at the head of Loch Riddon. (See pages 42 - 43.)

The Lucknow Gates: 3 km/2 miles along the glen, a replica of India's Lucknow Gates mark the former entrance to Glendaruel House, one time seat of the Campbells. Later redesigned by architect William Leiper, the house was bought in 1904 by William Harrison Cripps, who performed what is thought to have been the first appendix operation using chloroform. The house burned down in 1970.

The Lucknow Gates

Glendaruel Caravan Park occupies the grounds where Glendaruel House stood. It is a lovely peaceful site in the bottom of the glen. As well as holiday caravans for hire there is a camping lodge. Tents & touring caravans welcome. Open Apr. – Oct. (Vehicle access is via the A886.)

Home Farm Woodland Walk is a circular woodland walk past several waterfalls and from which it is also possible to climb Cruach Chuilceachan and on to picturesque Lochan Chuilceachan with spectacular views to Jura on a clear day.

Home Farm Cottages are the original Home Farm. The stable, coach house and dairy have been converted. Nearby was the Puppy House where estate dogs were reared.

The Watermill is a welcoming B and B which has retained many original features.

Campbell Mausoleum: Beyond the cottages, in a field, is a small mound where an 18th century mausoleum stands surrounded by trees. The mound is called "Dun an Oir", meaning "knoll of gold". Eleven graves are sited here, the earliest one dated 1727.

Earthworks

Earthworks: Evidence of ancient settlers is plentiful in Glendaruel. There are several burial grounds, cairns and cup and ring marked rocks. Earthworks can be seen from the road at GR006879.

The Glendaruel Highlanders is a tune written for the bagpipes by Alexander Fettes in 1860. It was adopted as the march past tune for the Argyllshire Volunteers under the command of Colonel Campbell of Glendaruel and retained when the regiment later amalgamated to become the Argyll and Sutherland Highlanders (Princess Louise's Own).

East Glendaruel Road (A886)

The A886 is joined by the minor road as it climbs out of Glendaruel and joins Caol Ghleann.

Dunans Castle: Once the headquarters of Clan Fletcher, a castle or mansion has stood here since at least 1590. Most of the present structure dates from the late 18th century. In the 1990s it became a hotel but was badly damaged by fire and left to deteriorate. It is now undergoing extensive renovation. It is possible to purchase a small area of the grounds, thereby becoming a nominal laird or lady!

Dunans Heritage Walk begins from a small roadside car park and takes in ancient woodlands, a ravine and a waterfall, a marshland boardwalk, Victorian gardens and a spectacular bridge.

Dunans Bridge was designed by Thomas Telford. Its height is unusual, the pointed arch rising some 15m/50' above the gorge down which the Alt a Chaol Ghlinne rushes to become the River Ruel further downstream.

The A886 climbs out of Caol Ghleann to reveal spectacular views of Loch Fyne as it sweeps down to the loch shore and the B8000.

EAST LOCH FYNE, KAMES & TIGHNABRUAICH

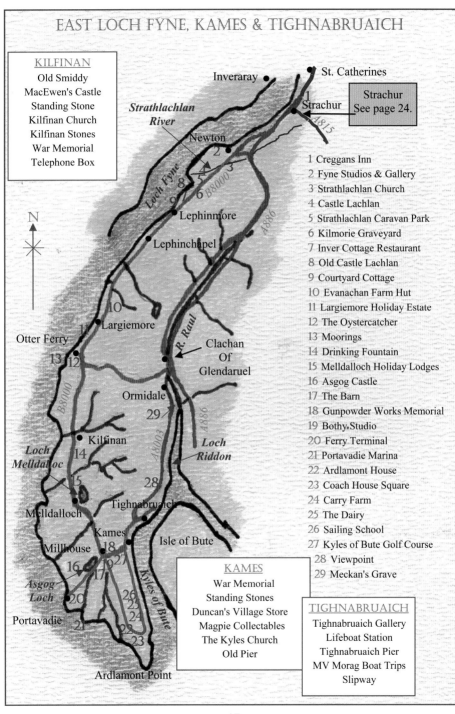

KILFINAN
Old Smiddy
MacEwen's Castle
Standing Stone
Kilfinan Church
Kilfinan Stones
War Memorial
Telephone Box

Inveraray
St. Catherines
Strachur
Strachur
See page 24.

Strathlachlan River
Newton

Lephinmore
Lephinchapel

Largiemore
Otter Ferry

Clachan
Of
Glendaruel

Ormidale

Kilfinan
Loch Melldalloc
Loch Riddon

Melldalloch
Tighnabruaich
Kames
Millhouse
Isle of Bute

Asgog Loch
Portavadie
Ardlamont Point

1 Creggans Inn
2 Fyne Studios & Gallery
3 Strathlachlan Church
4 Castle Lachlan
5 Strathlachlan Caravan Park
6 Kilmorie Graveyard
7 Inver Cottage Restaurant
8 Old Castle Lachlan
9 Courtyard Cottage
10 Evanachan Farm Hut
11 Largiemore Holiday Estate
12 The Oystercatcher
13 Moorings
14 Drinking Fountain
15 Melldalloch Holiday Lodges
16 Asgog Castle
17 The Barn
18 Gunpowder Works Memorial
19 Bothy Studio
20 Ferry Terminal
21 Portavadie Marina
22 Ardlamont House
23 Coach House Square
24 Carry Farm
25 The Dairy
26 Sailing School
27 Kyles of Bute Golf Course
28 Viewpoint
29 Meckan's Grave

KAMES
War Memorial
Standing Stones
Duncan's Village Store
Magpie Collectables
The Kyles Church
Old Pier

TIGHNABRUAICH
Tighnabruaich Gallery
Lifeboat Station
Tighnabruaich Pier
MV Morag Boat Trips
Slipway

The A83 Glen Kinglas road is joined by the A815 near Cairndow to follow Loch Fyne as far as Strachur. (See page 24.) Beyond Strachur the A886 is joined by the B8000 which runs down the wild and remote eastern shore of the loch, a single track road with very few settlements. The road passes through ancient woodland dotted with rowan trees and splendidly gnarled oaks.

Eastern Loch Fyne

St. Catherines

Until the 1960s a ferry operated between here and Inveraray - possibly not providing free passage for pilgrims and the blind as in the 17th century! The pier once enjoyed a regular steamer service to Inveraray, the Hell's Glen road linking with the steamer services to Lochgoilhead. The Ferry Inn, later to become St. Catherine's Hotel, dates back to 1460 but, sadly, is now derelict. The stone for Inveraray Castle was quarried at St. Catherines during the 1750s.

Creggans Inn

Creggans Inn, originally a coaching inn, has been refreshing travellers for centuries. For many years it was owned by Sir Fitzroy Maclean. His wife, Lady Veronica Maclean who was a renowned cookery writer, managed the kitchen. The hotel has a scenic outside eating area. MacPhunns Bar & Restaurant is named after "Half Hung Archie". Various legends tell why Archibald MacPhunn was sentenced to be hung. However, his wife saw his "corpse" twitch and revived him. Restaurant, bar meals, teas & coffees, accommodation. Open all year.

Newton, signposted from the main road 4 miles south of Strachur, is a pretty hamlet of white painted cottages on the shores of Loch Fyne.

Fyne Studios & Gallery: Artists Don McNeil and Jean Bell produce dynamic and distinctive Scottish art. Don works in oils and acrylics, his "Synchronicity" series depicting Scottish scenes in vibrant explosions of colour. Jean Bell's work includes cottages whose windows appear to be illuminated, an effect achieved by the inclusion of shiny toffee wrappers! Open daily.

Stachur - see page 24.

Strathlachlan

Strathlachlan Church: (GR021958) This lovely old church has an unusual, tiny bell tower. The church was built in 1792 and has a splendid organ, made in 1926 and gifted to the church by

Strathlachlan Church

MacLachlan of MacLachlan to commemorate local men lost in WWI. It is a chamber organ built by David Hamilton of Edinburgh, of a type often made for private houses or smaller churches and with a beautiful melodious tone.

Castle Lachlan is an imposing baronial mansion glimpsed from the road. Originally built in the 18th century, it was transformed to its present design a century later and is the home of the Clan Lachlan Chief. The family, descended from an 11th century Irish prince, still live here. As well as being a popular event venue, the estate offers luxurious holiday accommodation.

Strathlachlan Caravan Park is a tranquil holiday park in beautiful woodland by the Strathlachlan River. (No tents or tourers)

Kilmorie Graveyard

Kilmorie Graveyard (GR 012952) is an ancient Clan Lachlan burial ground. A church has probably existed here since the 8th century, although the present ruin dates from the 15th century, having been in use until replaced by Strathlachlan Church (see page 48).

Inver Cottage Restaurant is a restored fisherman's cottage in a stunning location on the shores of Loch Fyne. Home cooked local produce, coffee, tea and light meals are served all day, also evening dinner. Craft shop and gallery. Seasonal.

Old Castle Lachlan: A castle was built on the rocky headland at the edge of Lachlan Bay during the 13th century but the present ruins date from two centuries later. A path leads from Inver Cottage to the castle. An ongoing conservation programme is funded by Historic Scotland and The Lottery Heritage Fund.

Courtyard Cottage: (Letters Farm) Bob Brown uses acrylics, watercolour and pencil to capture the qualities of light in stunningly atmospheric, textured scenes. Open daily.

Evanachan Farm Hut

Lephinchapel was once the site of a chapel, now in ruins. Here the Lephinchapel Burn joins Loch Fyne after tumbling down a steep gorge 1 km/0.6 miles upstream.

Evanachan Farm Hut is one of the quirkiest and best self-service outlets in the land! A tiny roadside hut contains local produce including eggs, vegetables, cheese and home-made chutneys as well as lovely home spun woolly cushions, books for exchange… and much more. Open 24 hours in summer.

Largiemore Holiday Estate is a peaceful, family run holiday retreat with a small number of chalets and an annexe available for holiday lets.

Otter Ferry: The name possibly derives from the Gaelic "oitir", a spit of land. A ferry ran between here and West Otter on the far shore from the late 1700s. Remains of the jetty are still visible. The 18th century fare was 3d (old pence) for a man and 9d for a horse, no doubt considerably more by 1948 when the service ceased. During WWII a boom was laid across Loch Fyne here to prevent submarines penetrating the loch. From the beach at Otter Ferry it is possible to walk along the mile long spit at low tide. (Beware of incoming tides.)

The Oystercatcher

The Oystercatcher

The Oystercatcher is an atmospheric pub and restaurant in a stunning location, serving fine cuisine and specialising in local seafood including a wonderful Loch Fyne crab salad. Complemented by real ales, the menu is superb. Open 11.00 (12.30 Sunday) – 23.00 during the season. Booking recommended: 01700 821229. Well behaved dogs welcome. Visitor moorings are available for those arriving by boat (free to those dining at the restaurant). Wi Fi, bothy and shower block.

Kilfinan

The name derives from "Kil", a religious cell or chapel. St. Finan was a 6th century Irish missionary monk. The village is aligned to the Otter Estate, the seat of Clan Ewen of Otter (also known as McEwen or McEwan) and was once a community of almost fifteen hundred people but this declined at the end of the 18th century.

The Old Smiddy (smithy) can be seen by the side of the road.

MacEwen's Castle: On Rubha Beag, at the north end of Kilfinan Bay, stand the ruins of a former clan stronghold.

Standing Stone: A large diamond shaped stone, over 2m/7' stands by a wall just west of the road. (GR925794)

Kilfinan Church, dating from the 13th century, was erected on the site of a 7th century chapel. The present church was extended in 1633. The belfry, added in the mid 18th century, is a small, four sided structure known as a "birdcage belfry". In 1882 the church underwent restoration by renowned architect John Honeyman. More recent, restoration revealed medieval doors and windows covered up by previous works.

The Kilfinan Stones

The Kilfinan Stones, in a vault at the rear of the church, are amazingly well preserved burial stones, some from the 9th century.

Kilfinan Church

The War Memorial beyond the church is a simple cross.

The Kilfinan Hotel dates from the 1760s. One resident thought to have been there for much of that time is the ghost of a Lamont Clan member. The hotel is renowned for its warm welcome (literally - with cosy log fires and a plentiful selection of warming malt whiskies!), its fine dining and spectacular sunsets (best enjoyed with one of the Kilfinan's imaginative after-dinner cocktails!) There is a special guest book for members of Clan McEwen.

The Kilfinan Hotel

Public Telephone Box: Kilfinan's hospitality extends to its telephone box – thoughtfully provided with a chair!

Drinking Fountain: 2 km/1.2 mile south of Kilfinan a curious roadside fountain is dedicated to the memory of "Patrick Rankin of Otter and Auchengray, 1880". Fresh clear water, thought to have health giving qualities, spouts into a stone trough. This was possibly intended to quench the thirst of horses but now has two plastic cups for thirsty two-legged travellers.

Loch Melldalloch is a small loch with a wooded island.

Melldalloch Holiday Lodges offer tranquil holiday accommodation in comfortable lodges.

Asgog Loch: Just west of Millhouse, the Cowal Way leaves the road to pass this small loch, which was dammed to supply water for the nearby gunpowder works.

Asgog Castle (ruins) on the western shore of Asgog Loch was a Lamont stronghold which was besieged in the mid 1600s and destroyed by Clan Campbell after the 1646 Toward massacre.

Millhouse

The tranquil appearance of this lovely village belies its explosive past: From 1839 to 1921 it was the site of a gunpowder works, one of four in Argyll. Saltpeter, sulphur and charcoal were landed at Kames Pier and transported to Millhouse for manufacturing gunpowder which was then exported in barrels.

The Barn

The Barn is a real gem – a licensed take-away with a mouth-watering menu serving local produce, home baking and luxury ice cream. There is also a comfy lounge, kids' corner and a craft shop selling locally made aprons and bags, hand-knitted clothes, gorgeous baby bonnets and local artwork. Interesting old photographs line the walls. Open daily except Tue. Mar. – Dec.

Gunpowder
Works Memorial

Gunpowder Works Memorial: By the cemetery on the Kames road is an unusual and fitting memorial to workers killed in explosions at the works and also to crew members drowned in 1864 when the works steamer sank. The factory timekeeping bell is mounted above a small canon which was used to test gunpowder strength. Behind the memorial is a time capsule made up by villagers in 2007 and to be opened in 2107.

Bothy Studio: Two artists share the studio - Grace Donnelly who works in a variety of media, drawing inspiration from nature, and Jim Owens who produces evocative oil paintings of shipyards of the past. Open weekends. (Seasonal)

Portavadie

This was once a small fishing village. During the 1970s there was much controversy when a huge facility for constructing oil rig platforms was created, along with the village of Pollphail to house workers. The installation was never used and the unoccupied village fell into disrepair. However, fortunes have turned again for Portavadie with the construction of a huge modern marina. Nearby, fish are loaded into tanks for live transport and logs from local forestry operations leave by sea.

Lub na Faochaige

Lub na Faochaige is a delightful inlet near the tiny ferry terminal. There is a good beach, clear water, a picnic area and signposted nature walks. A popular walk from here is along the Cowal Way to Asgog Loch. (See pages 47 and 51.)

Tarbert Ferry

Tarbert Ferry: A small passenger and car ferry operates between Portavadie and Tarbert on the Kintyre Peninsula.

Portavadie Marina is a stylish marina with first class facilities and an excellent restaurant serving breakfast, lunch and dinner. There is berthing for over two hundred yachts as well as accommodation for non sea-faring visitors at the Lodge at Portavadie. Open all year. Tel: 01700 811075

Portavadie Marina

Ardlamont

Millhouse and Kames are separated by only 2 km/1.2 miles along the B8000. A picturesque alternative is the 12 km/7.4 mile single track road south from Millhouse to Ardlamont Point from where there are panoramic views towards Bute, Kintyre and

Goat Fell on Arran. The road then turns north to follow the shore of the western Kyles of Bute to Kames. The Ardlamont Peninsula is home to deer, badgers and various species of bat, while Loch Fyne and The Kyles Of Bute, are host to porpoises, dolphins, otters and the occasional basking shark.

Kilbride Bay

Kilbride Bay (also known as Ostel Bay) is a remote, white sandy beach, a pleasant 20 minutes' walk from the road. Parking is near Kilbride Farm. During WWII this beach was a training area for the D-Day landings.

Ardlamont House is a 16th century mansion which was the home of the Lamonts after the 1646 massacre when two hundred clan members were killed. It was the scene of another bloody murder in the 19th century when a young aristocrat was shot, allegedly by his tutor. The case was dismissed, "not proven" according to Scottish law, in spite of evidence by Dr. Joseph Bell, who was the inspiration for Conan Doyle's Sherlock Holmes. The house, along with several cottages, is now part of a relaxing holiday escape and function venue with fishing, stalking, horse-riding and carriage-driving (including for the disabled and autistic).

Coach House Square

Ardlamont Coach House Square, centred on the estate's former coach house, has a superb café with comfortable couches. There is also a quirky gift shop, roaring fires, a place to dry wet clothing and a menu including a range of buns, home-made pies and pasties with unusual fillings such as red onion and clotted cream. There is also a garden centre and a fascinating collection of old carriages.

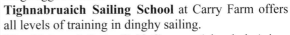

Coach House Square

Carry Farm, 3 km/2 miles south of Kames, is an award winning holiday park with its own stretch of shore. As well as lodges there is a limited number of spaces for tourers and camper vans. Booking essential Tel: 01700 811717.

The Dairy serves home baking and has a small craft shop selling knitting needles and hand spun wool from the farm's flock of Hebridean sheep. (Seasonal.) Free range eggs for sale.

The Dairy

Tighnabruaich Sailing School at Carry Farm offers all levels of training in dinghy sailing.

The Kyles of Bute Golf Course, (nine holes) is a fabulous, hilly course with burns and patches of heather instead of bunkers. Prepare to be distracted by the stunning views (but not always views of the next flag – the course has two blind shots!)

Kames & Tighnabruaich

War Memorial & Standing Stone

Kames

Kames was once a busy port. At "Black Quay" raw materials for the nearby gunpowder factory were brought ashore, originally from sailing boats but in later years from "puffers". Nearby stood a building where raw saltpeter was processed before being sent to the powder works at Millhouse. During WWII the large car park and slipway were built to accommodate tanks for training for the D-Day Landings. Kames accommodated wartime evacuees from Glasgow, many of whom still return for their holidays.

Kames Post Office sells cards, postcards, ice cream and all manner of useful hardware items such as light bulbs and paintbrushes. Cash machine.

The War Memorial at the crossroads is an unusual obelisk with a sculpted stone flag.

Standing Stones: There are three standing stones in Kames, one inside railings by the War Memorial and two opposite the post office. They are thought to be either the remains of a stone circle or the entrance pillars to a burial chamber.

Duncan's Village Store

The Kames Hotel

Duncan's Village Store: "Emporium" would better describe this wonderful, award-winning shop with its huge selection of groceries, local meats including venison, cheeses, wines & spirits, chilled goods, lottery and much more. Open daily.

Magpie Collectables sells antiques and bric-a-brac, including Wade miniatures, hand knitted woollies and much more.

The Kames Hotel is a traditional Scottish inn with a wood-panelled bar, fabulous views and a reputation for excellent,

locally inspired food. The selection of malts will keep the most discerning connoisseur happy, as will the wine list and the real ales – many of which are local. Visitor moorings available.

The Kyles Church is an attractive building dating from 1898. Built of grey stone, window frames and other features are picked out in red sandstone and the unusual shape of its windows give it an "arts & crafts" style appearance. The distinctive "belfry" is a free standing red metal structure.

The Old Pier, built by "navvies", is of unusual construction, the stones being aligned vertically rather than horizontally. It was once very busy: Herrings were shipped from here and there was a coal yard. It was also the disembarkation point for the servants of well to do families who used to travel by steamer to their summer residences. (The families disembarked at a separate pier from their employees.)

Tighnabruaich

Tighnabruaich stretches around a rocky shoreline on the western Kyles of Bute. Palm trees lend an almost tropical feel. The village has several gift shops and galleries, a post office, convenience store, bank, filling station, hotels, cafés and restaurants. As late as the 1960s Tighnabruaich was more reliant on sea transport than the road, the modern road link to Ormidale only having been constructed in 1969. Clyde "puffers" supplied most of the small community with all the essentials.

The Royal an Lachan

The Royal an Lachan is full of character with a reputation for fine dining, renowned in particular for its seafood menu. The welcoming Shinty Bar has photographs and other memorabilia relating to the Kyles Athletic Shinty Club, one of Scotland's premier teams.

The Burnside Bistro is open daily and has a menu which caters for all tastes and appetites, a wine list and a good selection of local beers. Outside tables provide a place to eat "al fresco" and watch the world go by.

The Tighnabruaich Hotel is a former 19th century coaching inn with spectacular views. Restaurant, bar, accommodation. Groups catered for.

Tighnabruaich Gallery exhibits contemporary original Scottish art, including that of local artist Jan Melfon, renowned for her vibrant modern paintings of yachts. The gallery hosts regular exhibitions by professional artists. Adjoining the gallery is The Tea Room.

The Rowan Tree sells a wide range of stylish gifts.

The Lifeboat Station houses an Atlantic 85 inshore lifeboat which was new in 2012 and which replaced an earlier Class 75. An RNLI

Jan Melfron

shop, open Mon – Sat, Apr – Oct, sells a range of lifeboat related gifts.

RNLI Station

Susy's Tearoom also sells ices and souvenirs. Coach parties welcome.

Tighnabruaich Pier, now "listed", is an attractive, well kept wooden 1830s structure originally built by the Castle Steamship Co. It has the distinction of being one of the very few surviving Clyde piers to still welcome a steam paddle ship - as one of the summer ports of call for The Waverley. The pier's history is told in the entrance hall and the old pier master's office, with photographs of old steamers and some original timetables.

Tighnabruaich Pier

MV Morag

MV Morag is a delightful, converted fishing boat offering boat trips from the pier along the Kyles of Bute with an interesting commentary on local history and folklore and, on longer trips, the chance to try angling. Tel: 01700 811 538 Mobile: 07799661493

The Wellpark Hotel is an exceptionally graceful, mid 19th century hotel built as a spa. The décor follows the "arts and crafts" style. The entrance hall and staircase are particularly elegant with stained glass windows. Dining is in the Victorian restaurant or the Edwardian lounge - a later addition to the original hotel. Emphasis is on freshly cooked local produce.

The shore road ends at a boatyard and slipway (use at own risk) but it is possible to continue on foot along the Cowal Way, round the headland Rubha Ban and follow the shoreline of the western Kyles of Bute.

National Trust For Scotland Viewpoint: The A8003 north from Tighnabruaich has spectacular views high over The Kyles to Bute and beyond. 2 km/1.2 miles north east of Tighnabruaich is a car park with a viewpoint indicator. It is possible on a clear day to see Great Cumbrae and, some 35 km/ 22 miles away, Goat Fell on Arran.

The Kyles of Bute from The A8003

Meckan's Grave is marked by an engraving on a rock at GR008807. Meckan, the son of King Magnus of Norway, was killed in a battle north of here at the foot of Glen Daruel. (see page 45.)

Ormidale House, 1.6 km/1 mile) north of Loch Riddon, was originally built in 1696 as the seat of Clan Campbell. It was extended in the early 20th century by Scottish architect Robert Lorimer and now offers luxurious self catering accommodation.

1 km/0.6 miles north of Ormidale, the A8003 meets the A886.

THE ISLE OF BUTE

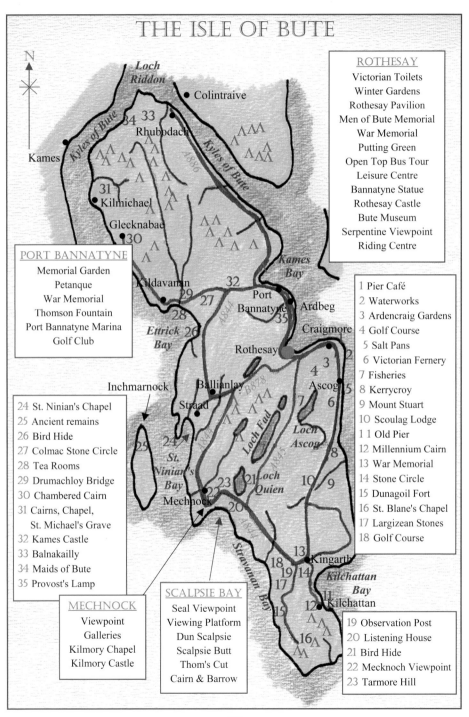

ROTHESAY
Victorian Toilets
Winter Gardens
Rothesay Pavilion
Men of Bute Memorial
War Memorial
Putting Green
Open Top Bus Tour
Leisure Centre
Bannatyne Statue
Rothesay Castle
Bute Museum
Serpentine Viewpoint
Riding Centre

PORT BANNATYNE
Memorial Garden
Petanque
War Memorial
Thomson Fountain
Port Bannatyne Marina
Golf Club

1 Pier Café
2 Waterworks
3 Ardencraig Gardens
4 Golf Course
5 Salt Pans
6 Victorian Fernery
7 Fisheries
8 Kerrycroy
9 Mount Stuart
10 Scoulag Lodge
11 Old Pier
12 Millennium Cairn
13 War Memorial
14 Stone Circle
15 Dunagoil Fort
16 St. Blane's Chapel
17 Largizean Stones
18 Golf Course

24 St. Ninian's Chapel
25 Ancient remains
26 Bird Hide
27 Colmac Stone Circle
28 Tea Rooms
29 Drumachloy Bridge
30 Chambered Cairn
31 Cairns, Chapel,
   St. Michael's Grave
32 Kames Castle
33 Balnakailly
34 Maids of Bute
35 Provost's Lamp

MECHNOCK
Viewpoint
Galleries
Kilmory Chapel
Kilmory Castle

SCALPSIE BAY
Seal Viewpoint
Viewing Platform
Dun Scalpsie
Scalpsie Butt
Thom's Cut
Cairn & Barrow

19 Observation Post
20 Listening House
21 Bird Hide
22 Mecknoch Viewpoint
23 Tarmore Hill

10. THE ISLE OF BUTE

Although physically a short distance from the mainland, Bute has an identity of its own. It is steeped in ancient, as well as more recent, history with the remains of many former settlements still evident. Bute passed between Norse and Scots before being finally taken under Scottish control in 1266 with the end of the Kingdom of The Isles. In 1400 Robert III made Rothesay a Royal Burgh. The Highland Boundary Fault passes midway through Bute, resulting in different geological characteristics at either end of the island, from gently rolling landscapes in the south to more rugged features in the north, divided by a band of red sandstone in the centre. The island boasts several sandy beaches and is a walkers' paradise. Two ferry services serve the island; one between Wemyss Bay and Rothesay, one from Colintraive on the Cowal Peninsula to Rhubodach, possibly Scotland's shortest ferry crossing.

Wemyss Bay: To The Ferry....

Rothesay

Rothesay is a charming reminder of a Victorian resort when people thronged aboard steamers to cross the Clyde, visit Bute's historic sites and enjoy its bracing climate. The promenade is a grand place to stroll with wonderful flower beds,

Rothesay Harbour

superb views and a wealth of interest. Faithful replicas of original cast iron lampposts bear the town coat of arms and are adorned with brightly filled hanging baskets. In the town centre are several lovely castellated buildings including the old sherrif's court and jail and several 18th century buildings. There are many nice hotels and guest houses – we only mention a selection.

The Ferry Terminal is the main point of arrival on the island with a frequent service from Wemyss Bay.

The Victorian Toilets (Gents) by the pier are a "working museum" and quite amazing! Built in 1899, the crest of the Royal Burgh adorns the entrance. These public conveniences demonstrate the extreme of Victorian taste for the ornate! The walls are of decorated tiles, the floor of ceramic mosaic. The urinals are edged with dark green imitation marble and are fed by glass sided cisterns

The Victorian Toilets

and gleaming copper pipes. The adjoining, modern ladies' toilets were added during restoration in the 1990s. Ladies may view the Victorian part – when unoccupied! Showers, towels, soap and postcards available.

Bute Berthing Company: Visitors arriving "under their own steam" (or sail or motor) will find serviced pontoons right in the town centre. Tel: 07799724225/VHF Channel 37.

Open Top Bus Tour: Departing from Guildford Square, the tour takes in Rothesay, Port Bannatyne, Ettrick Bay, Scalpsie Bay, Kingarth, Kilchattan and Ascog. An interesting commentary is included. Daily, May - Sep. 09.30, 11.00, 14.00 and 15.30.

The War Memorial records the names of the Rothesay residents killed during two World Wars. Where many Scottish war memorials are a statue of a soldier this one features an angel holding a cross.

The Putting Green is on the sea front, by the Winter Gardens.

The Men of Bute Memorial, by The Winter Gardens, is a memorial to men who died in 1298 under the command of Sir John Stewart. They were supporting William Wallace against Edward, "Hammer of The Scots", at the Battle of Falkirk. Every man from Bute died.

War Memorial

The Winter Gardens is a Grade "A" listed ornate glass and steel Art Nouveau structure, built as a 1920s concert hall. Fully restored, it is home to The Discovery Centre, Visit Scotland a cinema and café. The Discovery Centre has a vibrant collection of exhibitions, old fashioned sea-side amusements and

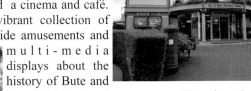

The Winter Gardens

Discovery Centre

multi-media displays about the history of Bute and its inhabitants, known as "Brandanes". One exhibition details the life of Greenock-born Henry Robertson Bowers who died with Scott attempting to reach the South Pole. Another famous Brandane, singer Lena Zavaroni, is also remembered. Open all year.

Alexander Bannatyne Statue: An imposing statue of one the town's benefactors (1838 – 1880) and Convenor of the County of Bute stands on the front.

The Victoria Hotel is reputed to be one of Bute's finest, in a wonderful location overlooking the water. Victoria's Restaurant serves a full à la carte menu while Ghillies Bistro offers a tempting, tapas-style mix of Scottish, Asian and Mediterranean food. Food served daily 08.00 – 20.45.

St. Paul's Church dates from 1854, its style "Gothic Revival". Stained glass windows depict Scottish saints, one of St. Paul and St. Peter with Jesus

Rothesay Pavilion, art deco in style and opened in 1938, is a grade "A" listed building.

It hosts live entertainment throughout the year, including a jazz festival each May.

Picture Bute, near the harbour, is run by wildlife photographer Philip Kirkham. In addition to stunning photographs, printed canvasses, mugs, T-shirts etc, the shop sells a wide range of original work by various Bute artists.

MacQueen's of Rothesay (butchers) make their own black puddings and sausages and is the sole outlet for Inchmarnock beef.

Glendale Guest House, built in 1830 to showcase ornamental ironwork available to adorn the homes of the wealthy, is an elegant and comfortable place to stay with an imaginative choice of breakfasts.

Beattie Court: This magnificent building at the corner of Glenburn Road was built as a Victorian aquarium, later to become a museum then public swimming baths and now converted to private apartments.

Beattie Court

The Glenburn Hotel is a magnificent building set in terraced gardens overlooking the town. It was built in 1892 as a hydrotherapy establishment.

The Esplanade Hotel is a large, traditional seafront hotel offering budget accommodation, bar meals and restaurant dining.

Trinity Parish Church, built in 1845, was designed in Gothic style by Archibald Simpson. Its square tower is topped with a tall, slender spire. Inside is an attractive hammer beam ceiling and stained glass windows commemorating the dead of both World Wars.

Rothesay Castle: Dominating the town is circular Rothesay Castle, Scotland's only round castle. It is largely intact with a drawbridge and a moat still full of water (popular with swans). The first castle to stand here was probably constructed at the beginning of the 13th century. It was seized and held by the Vikings until 1263 and much fought over in subsequent years. It became a royal castle when Robert II (son of Robert The Bruce's daughter and Walter Stewart) became king. Since then, the eldest son of the British monarch has taken the title Duke of Rothesay, as currently does HRH The Prince of Wales.

Rothesay Castle

Bute Museum

Bute Museum is a lively, interesting place. It is an independent accredited museum, meaning it can be awarded items through Treasure Trove and therefore has a collection of local archaeology of national importance. Items on display span the history of Bute from the early Mesolithic hunter gatherers up to the present. They include a rare Bronze Age jet necklace, a collection of inscribed slates from an early Christian monastery, the ship's bell from the S.S. Politician of "Whisky Galore" fame, a collection of model paddle steamers, a Punch and Judy and a wonderful set of brass weights and measures from pre-decimal days. The Natural History Gallery displays the flora and fauna of Bute and the Touch Table is a great favourite with children. The gift shop sells unusual books and cards, including a series of nature trails by the

Bute Museum

Buteshire Natural History Society. Open Mon. - Sat. 10.30 - 15.30. Sun. 13.30 -5.30.

Mercat Cross: At the junction of Stuart Street and High Street stands a replica of the mercat (market) cross.

Rothesay Leisure Centre offers swimming, sauna & gym facilities and aromatherapy.

St. Mary's Church, half a mile south of Rothesay, is the remaining chancel of the former parish church for northern Bute. The nave was demolished at the end of the 17th century to make way for a larger church, in turn replaced by the present United Church of Bute. Inside are two quite remarkable 14th century tombs, one of a knight, the other of an unidentified lady. The effigy on top of the Knight's tomb shows him in full armour. Outside the church is a finely detailed carving of a Christening.

St. Mary's Well can be found across the road from the chapel.

Canada Hill & Serpentine Viewpoint are signposted from the centre of the town. Canada Hill is allegedly so named because people came here for a last glimpse of emigrating relatives. The short but steep walk is worth the effort with superb views over the town, Rothesay Bay and the islands of Great and Little Cumbrae.

Ardbrannan Riding Centre offers year-round, all abilities trekking as well as riding and jumping lessons.

Roseland Caravan & Lodge Park is the only official camp site on Bute. It is beautifully situated on Canada Hill, overlooking the town and bay. Tents & tourers welcome. Seasonal

Craigmore

Craigmore's development as a residential area for wealthy Victorian businessmen is reflected in the architecture of its marine villas and mansions, one created by Alexander "Greek" Thomson whose designs often incorporated ornate balconies.

Craigmore Pier

The Pier: From 1877 Craigmore had a pier, the remains of which can be seen. Beside the arch leading onto the pier is a lovely old post box.

The Pier Café enjoys a spectacular situation on the old pier with stunning views over the water. Home-baking, filled rolls, hot meals, children's menu.

The Pier Cafe

Ardencraig Gardens contain a series of walled gardens and beautifully restored glasshouses, once part of the Ardencraig Estate but now owned and run by Argyll & Bute Council. Here plants are grown for Bute's stunning floral displays. Well worth a visit, the gardens are an absolute riot of colour. Open Mon. – Fri. 09.00. – 16.30. Sat/Sun. 13.00 - 16.30.

Ardencraig Gardens

Waterworks: On the front, beyond Albany Road, is a curious, ornate, crown-shaped building with the appearance of some type of defensive structure. Closer inspection reveals it to be making a whirring noise! It is, in fact, a well disguised water processing facility for Scottish Water.

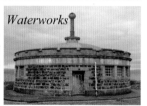

Waterworks

Rothesay Golf Course (18 holes) was founded in 1892 and is laid out around Canada Hill with spectacular views over the Clyde and beyond. It is a hilly course but ride-on buggies are available. The clubhouse serves food and drinks.

Ascog

The road hugs the coast through Craigmore and Montford with several parking places to enjoy the view before reaching Ascog, with its pleasant bay and beach. Rocks on the shore have been beautifully sculpted by the continuous action of the waves. A stone double-sided seat stands at a roadside viewpoint.

Salt Pans: On the headland at Ascog Point the ruins of 18th century salt pans have a chimney at one end and flues at the other. A plan to use locally mined coal to boil sea water to produce salt never materialised, possibly because the machinery for the scheme was lost when the boat delivering it sank!

Salt Pans

The Victorian Fernery: The Victorians were fascinated by ferns and in the grounds of Ascog Hall stands a wonderful glass and wrought iron sunken fernery, dating from around 1870, which had fallen into disrepair and become overgrown. In the 1980s the property was sold and, with the help of Historic Scotland and Edinburgh Botanic Gardens, the Fernery was restored to its former glory. Gardens and Fernery open Easter – Oct. 10.00 – 17.00

Victorian Fernery

Loch Ascog is a reservoir which supplies drinking water to Rothesay. It is also popular with anglers for its stock of pike, perch and roach. Permits from Bute Angling Association.

Loch Fad ("long loch") is stocked with rainbow and brown trout, alongside resident pike, for fly fishing. It was once Europe's largest trout fishery. Facilities include boat hire, shelters and toilets. Permits from Loch Fad Fisheries. Open Mar. – Dec. Tel: 01700 504871

Kerrycroy is a hamlet on the edge of the Mount Stuart Estate. A semi circle of quaint houses was built in 1803 by the wife of the 2nd Marquis of Bute as a model village for workers. The small harbour and pier were used to land stone for building Mount Stuart.

Mount Stuart: Built of red stone and centred around a majestic marble hall, Mount Stuart represents grandeur and flamboyance on a large scale. The present house was designed in Gothic Revival style by Robert Rowand Anderson for the 3rd Marquis of Bute. Building, which had begun in 1879, continued after his death. The lavish decor includes magnificent marble and stained glass, also priceless collections of art. Mount Stuart was the first home in the World to have a heated indoor swimming pool and the first in

Mount Stuart

(Photograph courtesy of Mount Stuart)

Scotland to be purpose built with electric lighting, central heating, a telephone system and a Victorian passenger lift.

In addition to the house and grounds, visitor attractions include a farm shop, children's adventure playground, courtyard tea rooms, picnic site, gift shops, garden and shore walks, a restaurant and a modern visitor centre with an audio visual presentation. House open: Apr. – Oct. 11.00 - 17.00 (last entry 16.00)

Scoulag Lodge, by the roadside, is a pretty white lodge bearing Stuart, Crichton and Windsor heraldic shields.

War Memorial: Between Kerrycroy and Kingarth is an attractive war memorial in the form of a Celtic cross.

Kilchattan Bay:

From Kingarth (see page 64) a minor road runs 2 km/1.2 miles to this windswept sandy bay with an intriguing history. A picnic area overlooks the beach. Nearby is a painted milestone and some traditional single storey cottages, one of which was the post office and another the police station, dated 1878. The road ends 0.5 km/0.3 miles beyond a stone jetty. Until the mid 1800s only a few fishermen's cottages stood here. In the 1840s The Marquis

of Bute established a tile and brick works using local clay. Initially unsuccessful, the tile works later produced over a million tiles annually. Increased competition and difficulties extracting the clay finally closed the works in 1915. By this time Kilchattan was well served by steamers and holiday homes had begun to appear. (Note the traditional double doors.)

Visitors' Moorings are available at Kilchattan for those arriving by boat.

The West Island Way, the 48 km/30 mile path which runs the length of the island, begins near Kilchattan.

The Old Pier: Built in 1822, the stone pier was an integral part of the local economy. Coal and other essentials were landed here and tiles and bricks exported (see previous page). Later, steamers brought tourists, while Irish boats landed workers seeking seasonal employment. By the 1980s the pier was in disrepair but has now been restored by the community. There is a car park, public toilet and picnic area alongside interesting information boards and a telescope.

Weather Vane: On a rock by the pier is a wrought iron weather vane, featuring a ship.

Kingarth

The southern tip of Bute is riddled with inlets and caves. This area is known to have been occupied from Neolithic times and is steeped in antiquity, with mysterious stone circles, remains of forts and an ancient monastery.

The Kingarth Hotel is a welcoming country inn, originally a croft house and established as an inn in 1786, with its own smithy. Food is served daily from midday in either The Old Bar, the outside courtyard or The Smiddy Bar with its cosy booths. Sailors especially welcome! Emphasis is on home-cooked Bute produce. The pub has its own bowling green.

The Kingarth Hotel

Black Park: 0.5 km/0.3 miles west of the Kingath Hotel, a minor road is signposted for St. Blane's Chapel. A short way along this road is a small parking area signposted Black Park for access to Kingarth Stone Circle and Largizean Standing Stones.

Kingarth Stone Circle: (GR:092557) Three stones remain of a Bronze Age stone circle. The stones can be seen close to the parking area.

Kingarth Stone Circle

Largizean Standing Stones: Three large stones stand in a row in a corner of a field at Largizean Farm. Their origin is uncertain but about 350m/380 yards away a set of bronze halberds were discovered.

Dunagoil Fort

Dunagoil Fort:"Dunagoil" probably means "fort of the foreigners". A path from Dunagoil Farm leads to the remains of this headland fort, thought to date from around 200BC. Vitrified walling can be seen – where

burning (probably following the destruction of the fort) heated the stones to such a high temperature that they fused together. Excavations discovered a substantial amount of Iron Age artefacts including jewellery, weapon moulds, a decorated bone whistle and tiny tweezers, all of which can be seen in Bute Museum.

St. Blane's Chapel: In the 6th century St. Catan arrived from Ireland to establish a religious community here. His sister gave birth to a child. Legend tells of Catan, in his anger, setting mother and child (later to become St. Blane) adrift in a boat which was washed upon Irish shores. St. Blane later returned to Bute and set up a monastery here. In the 12th century St. Blane's Parish Church was built here. A footpath to the chapel is signposted from the end of the road. Much remains of the church and its two graveyards, one for men and one for women, now in the care of Historic Scotland,

Bute Golf Club, founded in 1888, is the island's oldest golf club with nine holes stretching around scenic Stravanan Bay. Visitors welcome. £15 fee to be left in an honesty box. Booking not necessary except for parties of more than eight and on Saturday mornings.

Observation Post: Just south of the club house is a military observation post from the Cold War – used between 1961 and 1991. Beneath is an underground bunker.

Stravanan Bay: Back on the A844, the road meanders between fertile fields with views of Arran to the south west and, closer to hand, the sweep of Stravanan Bay which can be accessed along the West Island Way which is signposted. The beach is a mixture of sand and shingle. An interesting geological feature between here and Scalpsie Bay 2 km/1.2 miles to the north east is a raised beach – the original coastline clearly visible and marked by several caves some 0.5 km/0.3 miles from the present waterline.

The western side of Bute is beautiful, wild, remote and characterised by sweeping sandy bays separated by craggy headlands. The fertile soils give rise to many farms and dry stone walling is an attractive roadside feature, interspersed with vibrant wild montbresia and directions signed, as throughout Bute, by old cast iron signposts.

Scalpsie

Loch Quien Bird Hide is signposted from the road. In the loch are the remains of a crannog (a dwelling built on a small man-made island for defence). The loch is a favourite haunt of great crested grebe, renowned for their elaborate mating displays. Coots, barnacle and greylag geese, shelducks and swans also frequent the loch.

The Listening House

The Listening House: A small, innocent looking cottage by the roadside was used as a listening post to detect hostile submarines during The Cold War.

Scalpsie Bay

Scalpsie Bay: An excellent set of information boards, way-marked paths and viewpoints make this a fascinating place to explore. The beach is secluded and sandy, tinged reddish due to the underlying red sandstone. During WWII Scalpsie was seen as a possible site for invasion. Still visible are the remains of sunken timber posts - anti glider defences. The beach here is geologically interesting: Two different rocks meet - red sandstone and grey schist. West of the bay another section of raised beach (see page 65) has a sea stack (known as The Haystack) which would once have stood in the water.

Seal Viewpoint: A large colony of seals often bask on the rocks to the north of the bay at Ardscalpsie.

The Viewing Platform overlooks an area containing several interesting sites as well as enjoying panoramic views further afield towards Arran and Holy Isle. An information board details the various sites to explore.

Dun Scalpsie, situated on a hillock, is the remains of an Iron Age fortress. The entrance is clearly visible but much else has disappeared. During WWII two machine gun emplacements and a stone shelter were built among the ruins.

Scalpsie Butt is a bluff of land built as a division between medieval tenants' holdings.

Thom's Cut is a ditch which was once part of a network supplying water for hydro power for Thom's cotton mills at Rothesay.

Scalpsie Barrow can be seen in the field beside the parking place. Recent excavation uncovered a beaker to add to the Bronze Age food vessel excavated over 100 years earlier.

Tarmore Hill: A footpath leads here from the car park. Natural terraces were once used for agriculture. The short climb is worth the effort for the panormaic views over the Sound of Bute to the Isle of Arran.

Mecknoch Viewpoint (GR044594) The picnic table here is an idyllic place to eat while enjoying spectacular views over Inchmarnock, Arran, Ardlamont Point on the west Kyles of Bute and to Kintyre.

Ray Beverley (Mecknoch) creates unique and stunning wooden furniture, letting the natural characteristics of the wood determine his designs. To visit, Tel: 01700 500029.

Ruth Slater works in a range of media to capture the essence of Bute wildlife and scenery. Studio open Thu. – Sun.

Kilmory Chapel: Remains, although overgrown, can be seen of an ancient chapel. A lead coffin was unearthed here during the 19th century.

Kilmory Castle, at the hamlet of Meikle Kilmory was a small tower house, thought to have been the residence of the Jamiesons of Kilmory, local tax collectors.

St. Ninian's Bay: From the hamlet of Ballianlay a minor road forks off towards St. Ninian's Bay, ending at Straad from where a track leads down to the beach. An old water pump at the end of the road is a reminder of days gone by. St. Ninian's, another of Bute's sandy beaches, is usually littered with cockle shells. It is sheltered by a spit of land, St. Ninian's Point, which is cut off at high tide. In Autumn the fields behind the bay welcome thousands of migrating geese.

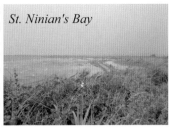
St. Ninian's Bay

St. Ninian's Chapel: The ruins of this 7th century Christian chapel are situated at St. Ninian's Point.

Inchmarnock is a flattish island off St. Ninian's Point. Privately owned and no longer regularly inhabited, it once had three farms, a busy shell fish industry and, until the 19th century, a slate quarry. The name is derived from St. Marnock who established a monastery on the island during the 7th century. The remains of a medieval chapel built on the original site can still be seen. A Bronze Age cist dating from around 2000BC was found to contain the burial of a high-status female of about twenty-five years old, known as "The Queen of The Inch". She was buried with a magnificent spacer-plate jet necklace which can be seen in the Bute Museum, along with a facial reconstruction recreated from a cast of her skull.

Ettrick Bay is one of Bute's larger bays with a long golden beach and clean water for bathing. Visitor facilities include two car parks, picnic tables, play area and café. At one time Ettrick Bay was linked to Rothesay by tram. The old tramway track has been turned into a path which makes a very pleasant walk from Port Bannatyne to Ettrick Bay with information signs along the way. Bute museum has published an illustrated Tramways Trail.

Bird Hide

Bird Hide: Ettrick Bay is a haven for many species of birds including stonechats and ringed plovers. A roadside hide provides identification boards.

St. Colmac Stone Circle: (GR045668) Eight stones remain of this stone circle near St. Colmac Cottages.

Drumachloy Bridge

Ettrick Bay Tea Rooms enjoys spectacular views over the bay. Meals and home-made cakes served. Open all year.

Drumachloy Bridge is a picturesque, hump backed bridge next to the modern bridge which carries the road over the Drumachloy Burn before it flows into the bay.

Kildavanan Point, at the western end of the bay, is a beautiful rocky headland with lovely striation scars on the rocks.

Kildavanan Point

Glecknabae: North of Kildavanan Point a single track road meanders 2.5 km/1.5 miles dramatically along the shore line, past shingle beaches and rocky outcrops to Glecknabae. Near the car park are the remains of a chambered cairn. The trees at Glecknabae are dramatically gnarled and bent due to continuous exposure to the wind.

Kilmichael is an archaelogist's paradise with several ancient remains. It is 2.5 km/1.5 miles north of Glecknabae along a track from the car park.

Cairnbaan, a 30m/33 yards long chambered cairn, is situated 700m/770 yards north of Glecknabae and is signposted off the track and up the hill past a waterfall.

Ferry Port: "Port" on the map is rather a grandiose description of a tiny inlet from where a ferry once operated between Kilmichael and Kames on the mainland. Nearby is the old ferryman's cottage.

St. Michael's Grave is a collection of rocks, the remains of another chambered cairn, thought to be between four and six thousand years old.

Glenvoidean Cairn: A further chambered cairn, all that remains are two upright stones with a flat one nearby which would have stretched across the top of the uprights. This cairn is up a track on the hillside above Kilmichael Cottage.

St. Michael's Chapel (Gaelic St. Maccaille) is an early Christian site, within a walled enclosure. People from Kames and Tighnabruaich would once be brought across to Bute for Burial – possibly because of the belief that ghosts could not cross water but more probably because it was easier to transport a coffin by boat. Legend tells of a sheepdog swimming across the water to be near his dead master.

North Bute

North Bute is sparsely populated. From Ettrick Bay the A844 crosses the island to Kames Bay to join the A886 which follows the rocky coast almost to the northern tip of the island. The area has retained a sense of being separate from the remainder of the island, in the past having thriving quarries and charcoal and fishing industries.

Kames Castle: Kames Bay boasts not one castle but two, this one having a tower, possibly dating from the 14th century with later additions and an 18th century walled garden. Traditionally this was the residence of the Bannatynes. Privately owned, some of the cottages on the estate are available as self-catering accommodation. It has an attractive lodge which can be seen from the road.

Wester Kames Castle is a 16th century castle which fell into disrepair but was restored in the early 20th century and is now a private residence.

Kames Bay enjoys panoramic views over the Kyles of Bute to the mountains of Cowal and beyond. At the northern end of the bay is a car park and picnic area.

Rhubodach: The road ends at the ferry terminal for the crossing to Colintraive. Lord

Attenborough owned the Rhubodach Estate until recently. Unusual lichen cover part of the jetty here.

The Bute Forest is community owned and includes Rhubodach Forest, part of the coastline and Balnakailly. It features way-marked paths and mountain bike trails.

Balnakailly is an ancient woodland, once part of a royal forest with some beautiful oaks, the remains of a 16th century farmhouse and a WWII bunker. An information board about Balnakailly stands at the ferry terminal.

The Maids of Bute (GR 008745) are a pair of rocks painted to resemble two women, thought to have been created over a century ago. Legend tells of two fishermen's wives, waiting for husbands who were lost at sea. They waited so long that they were turned to stone. More easily seen from a boat, they can also be reached by a rather strenuous walk from Rhubodach, not a long distance but over mixed terrain.

Port Bannatyne

Once known as Kamesburgh, the settlement developed in the early 19th century. A small harbour was built and a boat building industry developed. The name was changed when the Marquis of Bute bought this part of the island and renamed it for the Bannatyne family whose seat had been at Kames Castle. With the advent of steamer passenger services, the village developed as a quieter alternative to Rothesay with several elegant marine villas, a pier and a pleasant promenade with attractive iron lampposts.

Port Bannatyne Memorial Garden commemorates the 39 submariners who died between 1942 and 1945 serving with the 12th Submarine Flotilla based at HMS Varbel, formerly the Kyles Hydropathic.

Post Office and Tea Rooms: This is an old fashioned post office with a well stocked shop selling newspapers, lottery tickets, groceries, rolls & cakes from the local bakery, snacks & freshly made coffee. Cash machine.

Pétanque is a French game of boules. The village has strong connections with France and has its own pitch (or "piste") on the seafront. Boules can be hired from the post office.

The Port Inn is a traditional Scottish pub with a beer garden and pool table.

The Port Royal Hotel is a quirky place, once the village inn but now reminiscent of an imperial Russian tavern renowned for its range of vodkas. The bar is decorated with Russian artefacts and serves authentic Russian food, including breakfasts.

The Stone Pier, adorned with palm trees, has a shelter with seats – a good place to watch the yachts bobbing around in the marina.

The Anchor Tavern is a small traditional, sea-front bar serving light snacks.

War Memorial: An attractive Celtic cross sculpted with thistles remembers those who died in two World Wars. A separate plaque honours "the young men of the twelfth flotilla midget submarines" who trained on Bute.

War Memorial

Port Bannatyne Marina is a modern, hundred berth marina. Full marina facilties. Visiting boats welcome on pontoon D. To contact: Tel: 01700 503116 or VHF channel 37.

The Old Steamer Pier: Still visible are some of the timber supports of the former pier which was built in 1857 to accommodate visiting paddle steamers.

Port Bannatyne Marina

Port Bannatyne Golf Club has the distinction of an unusual number of holes – thirteen. Some holes are played twice before a separate eighteenth!

Kayak Bute: The waters around Bute provide wonderful conditions for sea kayaking, sheltered in the Kyles with open water beyond for more experienced paddlers. Tuition, day trips and longer expeditions. Tel: 07765 241686

(Photograph by Chris Stewart-Moffitt)

Ardbeg

Ardbeg is a residential area at the southern end of Port Bannatyne which developed during the 19th century. Several large detached houses from that era remain.

The Thomson Drinking Fountain: At the junction of Ardbeg Road and Marine Place is an ornate marble drinking fountain, erected in 1867 and identical to that in Glasgow's George Square.

Provost's Lamp: Outside a house on Wyndham Road is a Provost's lamp – a lovely red painted, cast iron post bearing the coat of arms on the glass lantern.

Ardbeg Bowling Club is a long established club.

Ardbeg Lodge is reasonably priced and incorporates The Striven View Steak House which serves locally farmed beef and lamb, including steaks and a home-made Bute beef steak pie. A full a la carte menu includes delicious home-made lasagne.

Ardbeg Point is a rocky headland, enjoying good views over Rothesay Bay and towards Loch Striven.

And finally …..The publishers would like to thank all those who have given so generously of their time and local knowledge towards this book, including the many people met and spoken with along the way. Special thanks to The Castle House Museum in Dunoon and The Bute Museum. The publishers would also like to acknowledge help received from The National Trust for Scotland, Visit Scotland, Historic Scotland and the staff of The Forestry Commission, The Loch Lomond & The Trossachs National Park and other organizations.

USEFUL INFORMATION

In emergency:
For Police, Fire, Ambulance, Mountain Rescue, Coastguard, Tel: 999 (or 112)

<u>Police Offices</u> are located at Dunoon, Rothesay & Inveraray. Non-emergency, Tel: 101
<u>NHS 24</u>. Tel: 08454 242424 (Subject to possible change.)
<u>Hospitals</u>: **Dunoon** - Tel: 01369 704341. **Rothesay** - Tel: 01700 503938
<u>Dentists</u>: **Dunoon**: Nigel Milne - Tel: 01369 702767. Dunoon Dental Practice - Tel:
0203 5141518. **Kirn**: Argyll Smile Centre - Tel: 01369 702755. **Bute**: Bute Dental
Surgery - Tel: 01700 502041
<u>Pharmacies</u>: **Dunoon**: Boots, Argyll Street. James Marshall, Argyll Street
Inveraray: J. W. McNulty, Main Street. **Rothesay**: Lloyds Pharmacy, Victoria Street.
<u>Vets</u>. **Dunoon** : J.A.Black - Tel: 01369 702532 **Rothesay**: Bute & Cowal Vets - Tel:
01700 503017
<u>Ordnance Survey Maps</u>:
Landranger Series. Scale 1:50,000. 55 - Loch Fyne, 56 - Loch Lomond & Inveraray,
62 - North Kintrye & Tarbert, 63 - Firth of Clyde.
<u>Bibliography</u>:
The Glory of Scotland - J.J.Bell; The Argyll Book - Donald Omand; Lochgoilhead, A
Slice Out of Paradise - Lochgoil Community Council; Memories of Dunoon & Cowal -
Renee Forsyth.